COLONIAL HOUSES

COLONIAL HOUSES
The Historic Homes of Williamsburg

by Hugh Howard

PHOTOGRAPHY BY RADEK KURZAJ

HARRY N. ABRAMS, INC., PUBLISHERS IN ASSOCIATION WITH
THE COLONIAL WILLIAMSBURG FOUNDATION

For Sarah Miller Howard

Acknowledgments

The Historic Area at Colonial Williamsburg is the most intensively studied eighteenth-century community in the United States and, very probably, in the world. What that means to anyone seeking to contribute to the literature is an unavoidable debt to those who have devoted their careers to examining Williamsburg's history.

While the research is thick with the findings of archaeologists, curators, and a range of historians, this book could not have been written without the members of the Architectural Research Department. The house histories offered here are based upon their investigations and observations, so I extend my particular appreciation for their time, good counsel, and deep knowledge to Edward A. Chappell, director, who offered me his unique insights into the James Geddy, Lightfoot, Palmer, and the Ludwell-Paradise houses; to William ("Willie") Graham, curator of architecture, who gave the tour at the Thomas Everard, George Wythe, Robert Carter, and Peyton Randolph houses, and shared with me the invaluable knowledge accumulated in his intensive study of those dwellings; to Carl R. Lounsbury, architectural historian, who generously spent time with me at the St. George Tucker House, helping me understand its remarkable and complex evolution; to Mark R. Wenger, architectural historian,

who revealed to me how many of the mysteries at the Nelson-Galt and Benjamin Powell houses have been unraveled; and, finally, to Peter Sandbeck, who provided a much richer understanding of the Tayloe House and the Coke-Garrett House. As the department's project administrator, Peter also proved an invaluable conduit. In person, as well as in their published writings (a number of their articles are cited in For Further Reading; see page 126), these five men put at my disposal more than eighty-five years of research assembled by members of the Architectural Research Department. Many of their insights and understandings appear for the first time in this book. I am in their debt.

The work of dendrochronologist Dr. Herman Heikkenen has also been essential, as the dating studies he conducted provide a baseline for understanding the houses of Williamsburg. Others from whom I have learned of Virginia's architectural history include contemporaries Travis McDonald, Dell Upton, and Camille Wells; from the past, my tutors included Sidney Fiske Kimball, A. Edwin Kendrew, Thomas Tileston Waterman, and Marcus Whiffen. These investigators, together with others too numerous to mention, have helped shape the study of architectural history in Virginia into a discipline that offers a rich and diverse window into the past.

Other people also helped make this book possible, in particular Joseph N. Rountree, director of publications, and Julie A. Watson, publications secretary. Thanks, too, to historian Kevin Kelly, editor Erin Michaela Bendiner, George H. Yetter, Louise Kelley, René Willett, Del Moore, reference librarian at the John D. Rockefeller, Jr. Library, and to copyeditor Richard G. Gallin who brought a close and careful eye to the manuscript. Thanks, as well, to vice presidents Richard McCluney and Cary Carson who provided institutional support to the venture.

At Harry N. Abrams, Inc., Publishers, Richard Olsen, senior editor, was the one who brought together the parties. Ellen Nygaard, senior associate art director at Abrams, is responisble for the book's handsome design. The staff at the Fiske Kimball Fine Arts Library of the University of Virginia in Charlottesville and librarians Peter Erickson and Nancy Spiegel at the Clark Art Institute in Williamstown, Massachusetts, helped me identify valuable secondary materials. Thanks, too, to my friend and agent, Gail Hochman, whose wit and pragmatism always remind me that publishing books is as much a passion as a business. And to Betsy, Sarah, and Elizabeth, whose ways of seeing consistently open my eyes to unnoticed nuance.

CONTENTS

Introduction

Williamsburg is an adventure in history of a most accessible and engaging kind. In the Historic Area, tourists in jeans and jogging shoes intermingle with shopkeepers and other costumed interpreters dressed in mid-eighteenth-century garb. The shops sell redware, the taverns serve peanut soup, the blacksmiths hammer out nails, and the shoemaker produces welted shoes. School kids, elder hostel groups, families, retired couples, and Japanese tourists come to gawk, to absorb, to learn; the sights they see are enlivened by horse-drawn carriages, picturesque gardens, and the sight of men wearing hose and tricorn hats.

If the streetscapes of the Historic Area at The Colonial Williamsburg Foundation constitute a sophisticated stage set, then the dwellings present smaller, individual *mise-en-scènes* for interpreting the history of colonial America. *Colonial Houses* devotes separate chapters to thirteen of those homes, original houses that have been extensively studied and, for the most part, restored to their eighteenth-century appearance. The oldest is the Nelson-Galt House, built in 1695; at the opposite end of the time line, St. George Tucker completed the transformation of his house a hundred years later. In the intervening century, Williamsburg citizens George Wythe (a legislator, jurist, and Thomas Jefferson's mentor) and Peyton Randolph (president of the Continental Congress) inhabited fine homes; tradesmen such as Benjamin Powell and James Geddy made their fortunes and sought social acceptance; and wealthy plantation owners such as John Tayloe periodically came to Williamsburg as part of the ruling class and resided in their *pied-à-terre* homes. These houses and others are featured in these pages, but to appreciate what they represent, a larger understanding of Williamsburg itself is in order.

Williamsburg's origins were humble. Many of its seventeenth-century settlers were former indentured servants who, upon earning their freedom, drifted northward from the colonial capital of Jamestown to the fertile tidewater lands on the peninsula between the York and James Rivers. An accidental neighborhood evolved, with a tavern, a couple of stores, a church, and two mills. Around the periphery of Middle Plantation, as the village came to be known in the 1600s, lived prosperous merchants and tobacco planters, while at its center the College of William and Mary was founded in 1693, only the second institution of higher learning (after Harvard) to be established in America. But it was a fire in Jamestown in 1698 that truly raised the status of the place. The following year the colonial capital of Virginia moved northward to Middle Plantation, and the hamlet was promptly renamed Williamsburg in honor of England's King William III.

The stage was set for a great eighteenth century. Williamsburg was a college town to which young men of means came to become English Christian gentlemen. The town had become the political focus of the richest and most populous of the thirteen colonies. The Royal Governor made his home there, and Williamsburg was the meeting place for the Governor's Council and the colony's lower legislative body, the House of Burgesses. One governor, Francis Nicholson, laid out a new town with a broad central boulevard (today's Duke of Gloucester Street) with the college at one end and the new capitol (built 1701–05) at the other. Williamsburg would flourish both as home to His Majesty's Government in Virginia and as a market town, central to the agricultural economy of the region. At a time when few towns in Virginia consisted of more than a courthouse, a tavern, and a handful of houses, Williamsburg aspired to a higher status with its many trade shops, taverns, and stores and its air of sophistication.

Prosperity was on the rise in the eighteenth century, and it trickled down the social strata. Life in Virginia had been a matter of subsistence for all but the wealthiest, but a growing number of people could begin to aspire to the refinements found in what was still regarded warmly as the mother country. England was rich, powerful, and many in Williamsburg sought to emulate its refinements in dress, manner, and culture. Successful tradesmen and small farmers of the "middling sort" could sit in their parlors and drink Chinese tea from cups made at English potteries. As the century wore on, men such as George Washington and Thomas Jefferson walked the streets of Williamsburg and talked in its taverns. Particularly during the "publick" time when the General Court met and the legislature was in session, Williamsburg was a vibrant place.

As the political ferment of the years before the American Revolution simmered, the place began to assume a more independent, a more self-consciously American tone. It is to the time immediately preceding the outbreak of war in 1776 that much of Williamsburg has been restored. The houses in this book for the most part reflect the appearance and character of Williamsburg in the last of its colonial days.

The demographics of 1770s Williamsburg are instructive. There were some two thousand permanent inhabitants in the city and perhaps two hundred dwellings. While some homes were inhabited by a single individual, others housed two dozen people or more, with an average of roughly ten inhabitants per dwelling.

Perhaps 15 percent of the householders were members of the professional or gentry class of the town—the lawyers, doctors, clergymen, college instructors, and the wealthy planters who served as members of the Governor's Council. A bit more than half of the heads of households would have been regarded as people of the "middling sort," artisans and merchants who, given

Williamsburg's principal way, the ninety-nine-foot-wide Duke of Gloucester Street

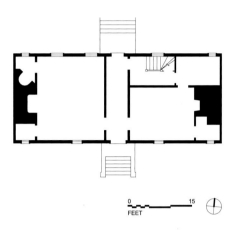

The Nelson-Galt House is an early example of a three-room floor plan with a central passage flanked by a hall and a chamber.

0   15
FEET

the urban nature of Williamsburg, prospered on and around Duke of Gloucester Street. Some of these even managed to climb upward in their lifetimes to the status of gentleman. The majority of Williamsburg's overall population, however, consisted of slaves (about half of the population of two thousand), along with a miscellany of whites of the "lower sort" who served as apprentices, tavern keepers, journeymen, and small-scale shopkeepers and artisans.

The two-hundred-odd dwellings in Williamsburg in the revolutionary era were, for the most part, one-story buildings, typically with two or more ground-floor rooms and habitable spaces above. Thirty-eight early houses still stand today, most of them the homes of the gentry and upwardly mobile tradesmen. While these dwellings represent the late colonial era in prosperous Williamsburg, they are not typical of colonial Virginia as a whole. Refined houses are always more likely to survive the ravages of weather, economic ups and downs, and changes of taste; and Williamsburg's well-to-do population had the money and motives to build houses with better chimneys and sturdier foundations than their country neighbors. More basic Virginia houses of the time consisted of little more than a wooden skeleton with a rough wooden skin applied, but the dwellings of the gentry tended to be larger and more stylish, so later generations found them more adaptable and appealing.

Room designations in the records of the time convey a good deal about the dwellings of the eighteenth century. The *hall* was a multipurpose room for eating, entertaining, working, and even sleeping (the usage of the word "hall" to mean corridor came at least a century later). The second downstairs room generally was referred to as a *chamber*. This smaller room would have been used for sleeping, though it often doubled as an entertainment space, where privileged visitors might have been invited. In some instances, the eighteenth-century appellation for this room was *parlor*.

In the 1720s and after, the hall-and-chamber configuration began to be succeeded by a more sophisticated arrangement in which a second partition at the core of the house produced a central passage (an early example is the Nelson-Galt House, see page 18, which was reconfigured early in the century). This third space on the ground floor served to limit access to the hall on one side and the parlor or chamber on the other, screening visitors so that social inferiors would be unlikely to gain entrée beyond the passage.

After midcentury another space appeared in more elaborate homes. The *dining room* would be the site for formal public meals and entertainments, which became de rigeur among the gentry and those who aspired to join the upper class (see the Thomas Everard House, page 36). The advent of the symmetrical Georgian plan introduced a fourth principal room on the ground floor, one typically used as a study, nursery, or second chamber (see the George Wythe House, page 44).

Each of these architectural changes held social implications, as a strict hierarchy governed who met with whom and where. Members of the gentry sought to live genteel lives, which involved excluding the householders' inferiors, not only slaves but also whites of lower social station. Such exclusionary practices conveyed a superior status to those members of the gentry invited to pass through to the privileged spaces of the house.

Today at Colonial Williamsburg a number of gentry houses are on display, but examples of plainer houses are rare. One that has been re-created is the kitchen quarter at the Peyton Randolph House, where the enslaved members of Randolph's household—those who did not sleep in hallways or in rough, unheated farm buildings around the periphery of the property— slept over the kitchen and laundry. Many less privileged people of the "lower sort" slept in houses with few comforts. Their homes had no plaster and lath but only a coating of whitewash on the inside surface of the thin exterior siding. Some of these dwellings had glass, but others just had wooden shutters. Such properties also would have had a garden that produced some vegetables—corn was a staple—and perhaps a few chickens or other fowl. It was a dark, cold, hard life, one that stood in stark contrast to the houses of the gentry and the upwardly mobile tradesmen who, in late colonial Virginia, established larger, more commodious accommodations such as those that survive at Colonial Williamsburg.

A domestic setting in Williamsburg in colonial times would have consisted not merely of a house with two or three or more rooms. A typical property for the gentry would have had a freestanding kitchen, perhaps a dairy, and not infrequently other buildings, including slave quarters, smokehouse, stable, and other domestic support buildings. The people who resided on the property might include not only the householder, his spouse, and children but also members of an extended family and a number of slaves. In the case of Peyton Randolph, who administered his agricultural holdings from his house on Nicholson Street, as many as twenty-seven slaves may have resided on the in-town property.

Walking the streetscapes at Colonial Williamsburg is one of the great pleasures of visiting the restoration. Given the circumscribed time frame, the fabric of the place is surprisingly diverse. Standing on Palace Green Street, for example, the visitor sees a familiar gable roof on the Thomas Everard House; across Palace Green is a double-hip atop the Robert Carter House; two doors south, the George Wythe House has a hip roof. A short walk east on Nicholson Street brings the visitor to a small building, an office at the Tayloe House; it has an ogee roof. And then there is the practically ubiquitous dormer in all its various incarnations. To make matters even more interesting, evidence has been found of long-obscured roofing treatments, as the Carter house attic contains the surviving roof framing from its original M-shape, while the Everard house has early clapboard roofing nailed to some of its rafters.

The shapes, surfaces, and forms of eighteenth-century architecture—the modillioned cornices, tall chimneys, handwrought ironwork, paneled doors, multilight window sash, porticos, beaded siding, and patterned brickwork—are pleasing. There are few signs of modern utilities and in the craft shops you do not hear the screams or whines of power tools. There is a quiet about the place, a simplicity, and, to some eyes, a purity in design and execution.

The Tayloe House, ca. 1950, before the nineteenth-century addition (right of photo) was removed during the house's restoration

⁂ ⁂ ⁂

Williamsburg remained the capital of Virginia for just eighty years. Thomas Jefferson lobbied in the early days of the revolution to relocate the capital of the Commonwealth. He had his reasons—it would enhance trade, he thought, since the population was no longer concentrated in the coastal region but had spread continually westward. Williamsburg's tidewater climate was regarded as unhealthy, too, and its location vulnerable to military attack. Within two days of becoming Virginia's governor in 1779, he got legislation passed that moved the seat of government to Richmond some fifty miles inland. Williamsburg began its descent into a century and a half of obscurity.

Ironically, Williamsburg's time in eclipse served its future very well. No longer of political or economic import, Williamsburg in the nineteenth century saw little excitement aside from a minor Civil War engagement on its outskirts. By the early twentieth century, it had become a backwater, its infrastructure outmoded with inadequate public utilities and its once grand thoroughfares rutted and ill adapted to the automobile. Yet as is the way with many well preserved early towns, its time in limbo also meant it was endowed with a rare lost-in-time

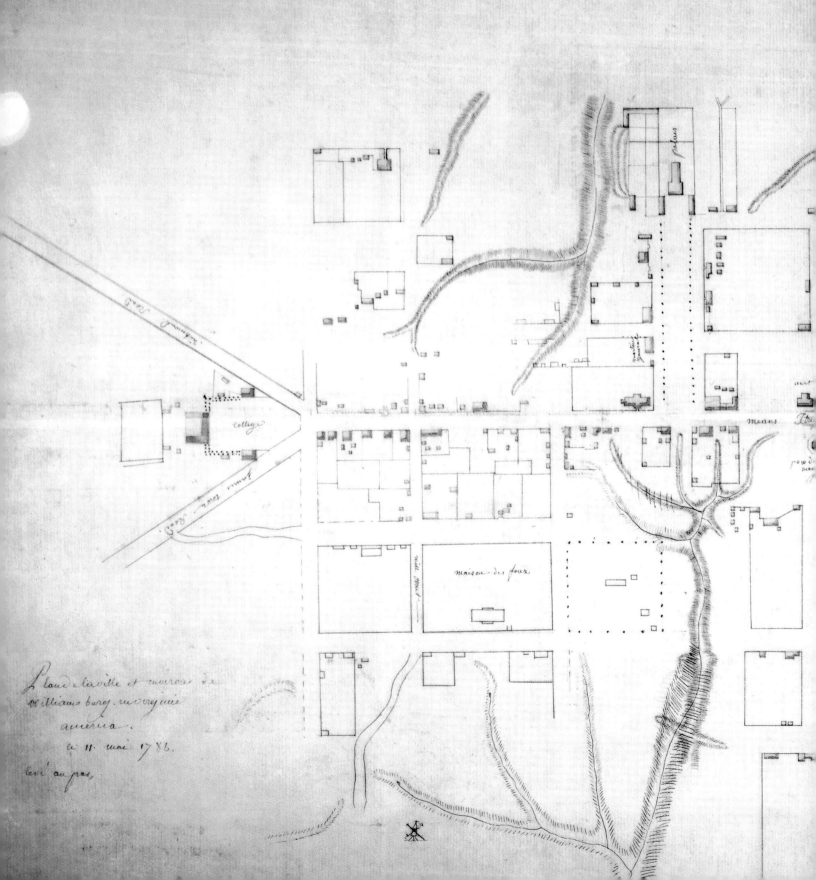

Plan de la ville et environs de
Williamsburg, en virginie
america.
le 11 mai 1782.
levé au pas.

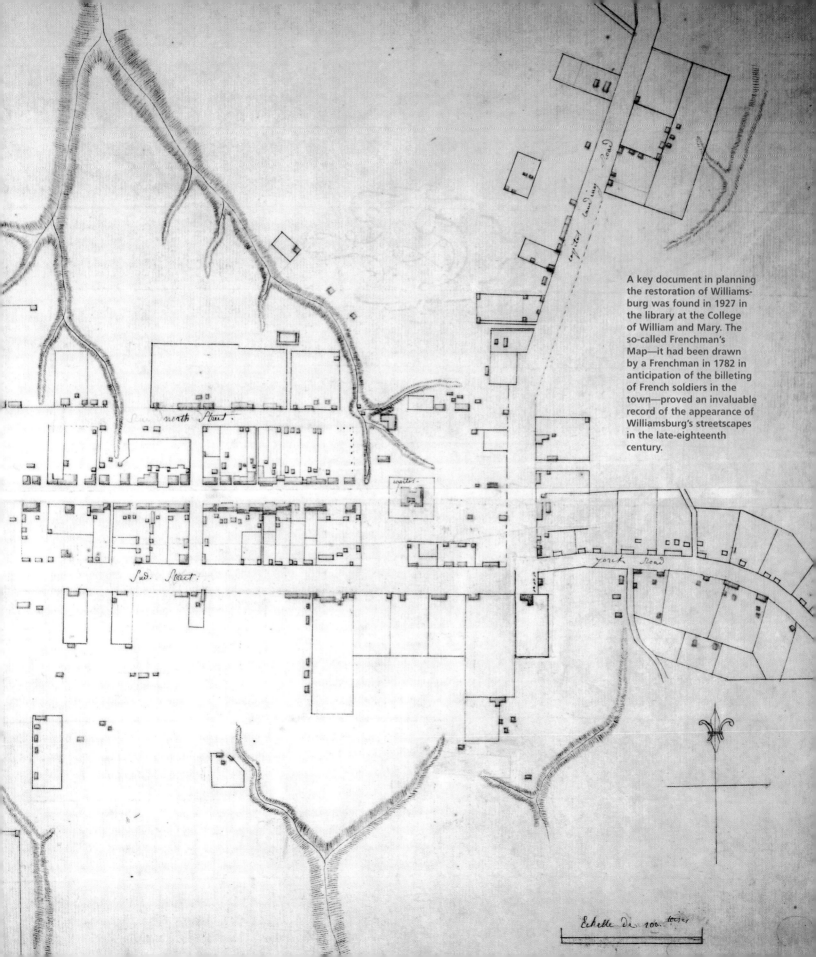

A key document in planning the restoration of Williamsburg was found in 1927 in the library at the College of William and Mary. The so-called Frenchman's Map—it had been drawn by a Frenchman in 1782 in anticipation of the billeting of French soldiers in the town—proved an invaluable record of the appearance of Williamsburg's streetscapes in the late-eighteenth century.

quality. Two men in particular recognized and sought to preserve that character. Instead of progressing forward, however, they devised another approach.

In 1905, Dr. William Archer Rutherfoord Goodwin had supervised the restoration of Bruton Parish Church. That task had given the rector the desire to do more, and when he returned to Williamsburg in 1923 from another posting, he had a plan not only for his church but also for the entire town. He managed to find a benefactor to underwrite the execution of his dream, none other than John D. Rockefeller Jr., heir to the immense Standard Oil fortune. Together they launched the unprecedented restoration that became "Colonial Williamsburg." Unlike other major colonial capitals such as Philadelphia and Boston, Williamsburg's streetscapes retained a surprisingly high proportion of eighteenth-century structures. More than eighty-eight original buildings were identified as having survived from the eighteenth and early nineteenth centuries. On behalf of the anonymous Rockefeller, Goodwin went on a buying binge, looking to acquire as much of the town as possible. Colonial Williamsburg, Inc., and its wholly owned subsidiary, the Williamsburg Holding Corporation (both formed in February 1928, four months before Rockefeller was revealed as the financial backer), purchased the houses and shops along Duke of Gloucester Street, as well as others. Eventually the restoration's holdings would incorporate most of the properties in the 173 downtown acres that constituted the core of the historic town. They were acquired house by house, deed by deed, block by block. Other properties in the public trust today include Bruton Parish Church, the Gaol (jail), Courthouse, and the Wren Building (home to the College of William and Mary). There also are two taverns, four shops, thirty-six outbuildings, and, of course, the thirty-eight houses.

The organization went public in anticipation of its formal opening. In August 1931, a booklet declared that the goal was to offer "a composite representation of the original forms of a number of buildings and areas known or, on good authority, believed to have existed in Williamsburg between the years 1699 and 1840." Key buildings that had been lost would be reproduced, including the Governor's Palace (destroyed by fire in 1781) and the Capitol (in 1832 it, too, had burned). The Boston architectural firm of Perry, Shaw, and Hepburn was retained to supervise the process, which involved not merely restoration of original buildings and reconstruction of lost ones but also the demolition or removal of hundreds of others. A federal highway was moved, streets resurfaced, and countless walkways, fences, lampposts, gardens, and outbuildings replicated.

The public was first welcomed in September of 1932 at the Raleigh Tavern, a reproduction of the meeting place to which Washington, Jefferson, and Patrick Henry, along with such Williamsburg worthies as George Wythe and Peyton Randolph, repaired for food, drink, and to talk politics. The reconstructed Capitol and Governor's Palace opened in 1934. President Franklin Delano Roosevelt arrived on October 20 of that year, dedicating Duke of Gloucester Street as the "most historic avenue in all America."

≋ ≋ ≋

Williamsburg has become a company town where people are paid to bring the past alive. Behind the scenes a coterie of scholars is constantly at work to assure that the backdrop for the reenactment is accurate; for three-quarters of a century, historians, archaeologists, curators, conservators, and architectural researchers have been studying and replicating Williamsburg's eighteenth-century context.

When the restoration opened its doors to the public in the 1930s, the houses, gardens, furniture, and even the Williamsburg color scheme fostered a revival of interest in colonial architecture and decorative arts. But from the very beginning, Goodwin wanted to do more than conserve antique architecture and artifacts: for him, Colonial Williamsburg was to be a tool with which to teach the sacred moments in America's past. As the 1931 booklet promised, the goal was to "supply a shrine where great events in early American history and the lives of many of the men who made it may be visualized in their proper setting." The original notion as conceived by W. A. R. Goodwin and Rockefeller was both pedagogical and political: they wanted to educate Americans about the nation's origins; by doing so, the founders wanted to convey a sense of connectedness to the values and the virtues of the Founding Fathers.

Colonial Williamsburg opened to the public during the depression, offering an admiring look back at the noble experiment in American democracy as it had been conducted by rich and important white men. The original interpreters, then called hostesses, were well-to-do white women who brought a similar air of gentility and heritage. They were greeting and educating their social and racial peers—initially it was the gentry of the twentieth century that came to examine the life of the gentry two centuries earlier.

The audience began to change in Williamsburg's second decade. Courtesy of Mr. and Mrs. Rockefeller, thousands of servicemen and -women were given carefully choreographed tours of Williamsburg during World War II. They heard a history lecture, watched a film, and saw the town, with appropriate stops at patriotic sites. After the war, this generation produced the baby boom, and not a few of those same soldiers came back with their young families. One result was that during the cold war years, Williamsburg gradually evolved into a middle-class experience, a vacation destination that offered food, lodging, and a digestible dose of education. According to the *New York Times*, by 1948 Colonial Williamsburg had become "a wise investment in the re-education of Americans." Yet the interpretation continued to be a closely circumscribed view of the past—for example, the half of Williamsburg's eighteenth-century population that had consisted of enslaved African-Americans was largely ignored in the interpretation of the time. Williamsburg itself in the 1950s was segregated, and most accommodations, restaurants, and public conveniences remained whites-only.

A more sophisticated and inclusive view of the eighteenth century has evolved. Colonial Williamsburg has become a part of our collective cultural memory, helping establish what has been called the American revival style, and continuing to portray the past of the place in patriotic terms. But the interpretation has grown very much richer, too. Members of the gentry and tradesmen have long been costumed and given roles to play, but more recently a more diverse mix of other documented historic figures, including the enslaved, has emerged from obscurity. The result is a composite glimpse recounted not only in terms of buildings and artifacts but also through personal narratives. Colonial Williamsburg has long been a cultural landscape; now it is a peopled place with countless stories to tell.

One way to experience Colonial Williamsburg is to walk its streets, to listen to its interpreters, and to enter its houses. Another approach is take the armchair tour offered by this book. Thirteen important and meticulously restored houses are profiled in the chapters that follow; their exteriors, plans, and individual histories are explored and examined in words and images. What emerges is a sense of the social and architectural history of the colonial era, a time with its own notions of order, pace, beauty, and law, all of which informed the establishment of our country. By examining these homes, a new appreciation can be reached of the enduring blend of elegance and simplicity that are the essence of colonial style.

FACING PAGE: Peyton Randolph would be the first president of the Continental Congress; his bookcases suggest the extent of his considerable library, then one of the largest in Williamsburg.

Nelson-Galt House

FRANCIS STREET
CONSTRUCTED 1695; RELOCATED AND ENLARGED AFTER 1707
REMODELED AFTER 1750

Each of Williamsburg's historic homes has its share of little mysteries, but the Nelson-Galt House presents an unusual one. *Whence, researchers are still wondering, came this house?* The question arises because at least a portion of this modest dwelling probably was dragged to its present site from someplace else.

The story reveals a good deal about how architectural historians at Colonial Williamsburg learn about individual buildings. One way to begin is by examining documentary records. In the case of this property, surviving deeds revealed that there was no house on the corner of Blair and Francis Streets when two adjoining lots were granted to one William Robertson in 1707. His deed, however, came with the then-standard proviso that "He Shall build within 24 months one or more good dwelling houses according to [the] Act of Assembly 1705." Robertson was a substantial member of Williamsburg society, serving as clerk of the Governor's Council, the upper legislative body in Virginia. Probably he did as he was required, and within two years, a house stood on the property. A further examination of deeds and documents revealed that the house was later owned for long periods by the Nelson family. Since they owned it before and after the revolution, and Colonial Williamsburg purchased it from the Galts,

the dwelling came to be referred to as the Nelson-Galt House.

Documentary evidence could take the investigation only so far—records from the early eighteenth century are incomplete—so the architectural investigators looked closely at the artifact itself. Every house is a treasure trove of physical evidence, and by examining the parts of this building—everything from its foundation to its roof, including the floors, doors, windows, nails, plaster, hardware, and virtually every other element of its structure and finish—a great deal was learned about its history and building chronology. The story of the Nelson-Galt House took an enigmatic turn when it came to a close analysis of the building's frame.

In 1990, a study of the building's frame was undertaken using a method of archaeometric analysis called dendrochronology. Every schoolchild knows that counting the rings in a tree trunk reveals its age, but a dendrochronologist takes that knowledge a step further. Not all growth rings are the same, since each varies depending upon growing conditions in a given year. Once the individual rings have been precisely measured, their sequence in a given timber then can be compared to a database of previously recorded ring patterns in timbers of the same species, from the same area, and of known ages. In dating a structure, then, the dendrochronologist seeks

FACING PAGE: Half-hidden behind a fence, the house is a private residence, not open to the public as a museum house. But even from the exterior, the hierarchy of the spaces can be "read" by looking at the various window sizes. The twenty-four-light windows illuminate the two main rooms of the ground floor, while fifteen-light windows light the more modestly sized rooms of the second floor. Eight-light windows brighten the first-floor closets at the ends of the house.

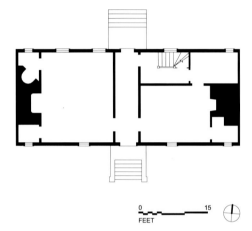

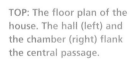

0   15
FEET

to determine the last year of tree growth, which indicates the time at which the timber was felled and used as a building material.

At the Nelson-Galt House, the findings were a revelation. The house, the researchers discovered, does not date from William Robertson's ownership after 1707, but it is actually a decade or so *older*, having been built in 1695. Robertson very likely purchased the property, acquired a house nearby, and had it moved to its new site, perhaps in 1707 or 1708. Thus, the house actually predates the formal establishment of the town of Williamsburg by several years.

Thanks to a few small specimens drilled out of its timbers, the Nelson-Galt House emerged as not only the oldest dwelling in town but also the oldest frame house in Virginia.

In its earliest incarnation, the house was 20 feet wide and some 37½ feet long, not including the exterior chimneys at each gable end. The main floor was divided by a partition into two unfinished rooms. The larger hall would have been a multipurpose space where much of the life of the house was lived—cooking, eating, working, socializing, and, for some members of the household, perhaps even sleeping. The second room, or chamber, opened off the hall and would have been a more private space, perhaps used as a master bedroom. Reached by a stair were two more chambers on the upper level.

Twice during the eighteenth century the house was significantly remodeled. Robertson resettled the original wood-frame structure on a new foundation. He extended the building about eleven feet to contain the new chimneys constructed at each end within the envelope of the house, along with four closet spaces, one at each corner, flanking the chimneys. Plaster was applied to the interior walls, sash windows introduced to the main floor, and dormers were added,

TOP: The floor plan of the house. The hall (left) and the chamber (right) flank the central passage.

BOTTOM: The individual parts are uncomplicated— a hooded center entrance, a matched pair of windows, and the delicate shadow lines cast by the cornice and weatherboards—but they come together to form a satisfying and appealing house.

three on each side of the roof. Half a century later, during the third quarter of the eighteenth century under the Nelson ownership, more changes were made, among them a new floor, paneled wainscot, and a stone mantel. In the course of both renovations, interior partitions were changed. The once standard hall-and-chamber configuration was evolving in Virginia with the addition of a second partition at the core of the house. The result was a central passage, effectively a corridor that served to limit access to the rooms on either side. In Williamsburg, social status was important, and the floor plan reflected the social hierarchy: social inferiors might gain entrée to the passage, but only the privileged few would penetrate to the private spaces where the finest finishes in the house (chimney pieces and paneling, for example) and objects (such as carpets and furniture) would be on display.

The Nelson-Galt House may seem small to us today—after all, it is two rooms up, two rooms down, plus stairs and hallways—but it was a house that only a wealthy member of the Virginia gentry would have been able to afford in the eighteenth century. Thomas Nelson, its owner for many years, was a major Virginia figure, having been a signer of the Declaration of Independence, a Revolutionary War general, and later governor of Virginia. In fact, this not-so-large house may have appeared even more modest when Nelson was at home, as John Adams once described him as "a fat man… [though] alert and lively for his weight."

Colonial Williamsburg restored this house in the early 1950s, removing a later wing at the rear of the house and making many repairs. It is now a private residence and not open to the public, but has survived surprisingly intact from the eighteenth century, with an important story to tell about the town's development in its earliest days. ◮

TOP AND MIDDLE: The gracefully curved brackets that support the door hood date from the eighteenth century. Though a reconstruction, the pedimented roof was fabricated based on evidence found in the framing and on the wall. It is a practical as well as pleasing addition, as it shields the entrance from the weather.

BOTTOM: A cornice with modillion blocks lines the north and south elevations of the house. Most of it is thought to be original to the late-eighteenth-century remodeling, though the crown molding beneath the shingles is a reproduction. Note, too, the beaded weatherboarding and shaped endboard.

FACING PAGE: The simple gable roof is made more interesting by the chimney and, in particular, by the trio of dormers with their hip roofs.

This room was transformed in the renovation shortly before the revolution, when the paneled wainscot, cornice, and blind-nailed flooring were installed. At the same time, the stone mantel was inserted, the firebox having been reduced in size. The mantelpiece is a reproduction based upon fragments found in the hearth.

When acquired by Colonial
Williamsburg, the house had
a two-story wing to the rear.
During the 1951–52 restoration, the wing, along with
other later additions, was
removed to reveal the more
modest earlier house.

At Colonial Williamsburg, some of the charm derives from the accretion of details such as the paneled window shutter, the suspended lamp, the strap hinges, and the louvered shutter door at this entry to the Nelson-Galt House.

Peyton Randolph House

NICHOLSON STREET

CONSTRUCTED 1715–18; REMODELED AND WING ADDED 1754–55

Beyond Williamsburg's boundaries, the name Peyton Randolph is largely unknown. In his time, however, he was a power in Virginia politics as speaker of the House of Burgesses and as one of the first leaders of the revolutionary cause. Randolph achieved national standing, having been unanimously elected president of the first Continental Congress in 1774. The next year he was reelected, but the portly patriot died suddenly of an "apoplectic stroke" at age fifty-three, just eight months before the signing of the Declaration of Independence.

Along Nicholson Street today the name Peyton Randolph endures as more than the answer to the trivia question, *Who's the forgotten founding father?* His house outlived him, a backdrop for the activities on Market Square and the Courthouse where Randolph had practiced law. It has also proved to be an enduring restoration laboratory for the study of early Williamsburg architecture, society, and material culture.

The original house was constructed 1715–18 for the same William Robertson who lived in the Nelson-Galt House (see page 18). He apparently never lived in the Nicholson Street house, renting it to tenants until 1723 when he sold it to John Holloway who, in turn, sold it to Peyton's father, Sir John Randolph, seven months later. Perhaps the most distinguished lawyer of his time in Virginia, Sir John was the only native-born Virginian to be knighted. Yet neither he nor Robertson seem to have finished plastering or trimming the interior of the house. That was left to his son, Peyton, who took up residence in the early 1750s when he came into his inheritance after his father's death. The house he inherited was a two-story cube. The main floor was divided into unequal quadrants, with the smallest space being the entry that provided access to the two public rooms, a hall and a dining room, both of which in turn led to a bedchamber in the final corner of the square footprint. Each of these three sizable rooms had its own fireplace, as did the three chambers above, which were reached via stairs in the entry. The Randolph house was grand for its place and time, since dining rooms were rare in early Virginia, as were dwellings with two full stories.

By the time Peyton Randolph took up residence in his widowed mother's home, he had completed his legal training at the Inns of Court in London; become Virginia's attorney general (at twenty-two); and married well, taking Elizabeth Harrison of Berkeley plantation for his wife. He set about applying new finishes to the house, adding plaster to the ceilings, paneling to many of the walls, and wallpaper in one room. A few years later (after his mother's death), he embarked on a second remodeling, this time adding a wing to the east side. Although the addition effectively doubled the volume of the house, only two new living spaces were added, along with a new stair passage or hallway, as we know it today. But the effect was to raise significantly the status of the house.

FACING PAGE: Peyton Randolph was a man of property, one held in high regard by his neighbors. In fact, the imposing character of the man (and his house) led some of his contemporaries to refer to his home as "Mr. Attorney's house."

TOP: Before its restoration, the Peyton Randolph House was almost unrecognizable behind its picket fence and richly detailed two-story porch.

BOTTOM: The original house consisted of only the first three bays, terminating between the third window and the Nicholson Street entrance in this photo. The original entrance was on the west elevation (near the corner in this image) and faced onto North England Street. The 1754–55 addition to the east added grand spaces inside, including a generous passage with a dramatic staircase.

FACING PAGE: The 1754–55 addition incorporated a new entrance and the seven windows on the two-story structure in the foreground. The smaller structure visible beyond is an earlier tenant house that, though it abuts the Randolph house, remained a separate dwelling.

LEFT: After 1715, the original house rose from a square footprint on the southwest corner of the property (lower left). In the mid-1750s, a wing was erected to the east, adding the stair passage and dining room to the ground-floor plan. Attached dependencies to the rear included the "covered way," a corridor and storage space that allowed indoor access between the main living areas of the house and the "kitchen-quarter," the large structure that contained the kitchen, laundry, and slave quarters.

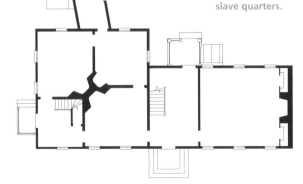

0   15
FEET

From the street, the updated house was more impressive, three bays having become seven. The original boxy structure had been transformed, part of a grand, symmetrical statement, with its center entrance flanked by three bays of windows on each side. When welcomed within, guests entered a large passage with an imposing stair lit by a large compass-headed window that overlooked the rear of the house. The large new dining room would have impressed guests, too, with its fancy marble mantel and two built-in cupboards. On the upper level, the Randolphs' personal quarters improved, with a new chamber for sleeping and, for the time, an extraordinary *three* closets. As the highly structured society of the era demanded, they could hold sophisticated entertainments consistent with their high station.

Just as the Randolph house was the site of periodic construction before the revolution, it was the subject of no less than four restoration efforts in the twentieth century. The first restoration was undertaken by a private owner; the second after Colonial Williamsburg acquired the property in 1938; and the third before the opening of the house to the public in 1968. But it was the latest (and ongoing) revisiting of the Randolph house that produced the most dramatic changes.

In the 1990s, new mechanical systems were installed and the failing roof covering was replaced. The interior of the house was reexamined, too, and the full complement of closets restored. The greatest changes, however, were outside and to the rear of the house where what was probably Williamsburg's most extensive domestic compound had been lost.

Its reconstruction was made possible by archaeologists who sifted through soil layers to comprehend the evolution of buildings on

Randolph decorated his central passage, pictured here from the upstairs landing, with architectonic "paper hangings" (wallpaper) in a "pillar and arch" pattern. Randolph could glimpse the workings in his extensive outbuildings through the "compass headed" window that overlooked his rear yard.

the site, along with paleobotanists seeking seeds and other minute plant remains. In the house itself, dendrochonologists dated various wooden elements, while paint analysts subjected layers of paint and finish to microscopic and chemical studies to reveal the chronology of the plaster, paints, and wallpapers. Aided by new physical evidence, historians were then able to seek other clues in the deeds, diaries, letters, and other documents that suddenly could be seen in a new light.

What emerged from the research was that Peyton Randolph had reconfigured his backyard at the same time he added the east wing. The result was a complex of buildings that extended well back from the main house. A fifty-foot-long covered corridor linked a large building that housed the kitchen, laundry, and possibly a servant's hall with slave quarters above. Other buildings included a smokehouse and a dairy. Further back on the property was a stable large enough for a dozen horses and two carriages, as well as

several storage buildings, including a granary. Plus there were gardens and pasture for grazing animals.

The missing buildings are being replaced. The covered way and the kitchen/laundry quarters have been completed. They were built by Colonial Williamsburg craftsmen, using materials fabricated in just the fashion they would have been in the eighteenth century—timbers hewn and sawn by hand, nails and hardware from the blacksmith shop, and bricks made nearby at the brick-maker's yard. The process has been witnessed by visitors to the Historic Area who marvel at the tools, the craftsmanship, and the amount of work required to raise a building as it was done in the handmade age.

Today the home of the wealthy and influential Peyton Randolph remains front and center; but the reconstruction of domestic buildings to the rear has made it possible to represent the lives of those other than the man of the house. As restored and interpreted today, the site constitutes more than a series

The east bedchamber on the second floor may have been occupied by Betty and Peyton Randolph. The elaborate bed, complete with its hangings, mattresses, and carved cornice, was appraised at £22.10, an extraordinary amount for the time.

of period rooms; a visit offers an opportunity to see beyond the luxurious spaces where Peyton and Betty welcomed their guests and their commodious private quarters.

By walking out the back door and the "covered way," one steps suddenly onto a very much lower rung on the social ladder. The meaner and distinctly unfashionable spaces out back represent the working and living areas for the slaves, rooms without paneling or fine furniture. In Randolph's time, most of the twenty-seven slaves believed to have lived on the property slept in the outbuildings, though several personal servants may have had designated sleeping spaces in the main house. In contrast to the genteel calm in the Randolphs' dwelling, its backyard would have been busy with the work of preparing food, washing clothes, and performing a wide range of domestic work. The Randolph house today suggests the interdependence of the Randolphs and their slaves. No longer is Mr. Attorney's house a stage set for an American revival view of eighteenth-century architecture and decorative arts. The portrayal now includes harsher and less savory elements of a highly stratified society in which class and racial differences defined and limited the prospects of all but a few. The Randolphs were among the most visible and influential families in colonial Virginia, and today their house once again resembles the establishment they knew. ᐊᐃ

The reconstructed kitchen and slave quarter to the rear of the main house, which housed the laundry, kitchen, and living accommodations for numerous house slaves

TOP: On the ground floor of the quarter, meals for the Randolphs were cooked in this kitchen. That is a food safe on the left; along the rear and right-hand walls is a waist-high work counter, called a dresser, where food preparation was done. Tables like the one at center were listed in the inventory prepared at the time of Peyton Randolph's death.

BOTTOM: This room upstairs with unfinished walls was actually more spacious than most slave accommodations. Peyton Randolph's manservant and his wife might have slept in the double bedstead, while the children would have slept on moveable pallets on the floor.

Thomas Everard House

PALACE GREEN STREET

CONSTRUCTED 1718; REAR WINGS ADDED CA. 1720

INTERIOR REMODELED CA. 1750 AND 1770

Thomas Everard lived the American dream. An orphan with no prospects who arrived in prerevolutionary Virginia in the 1730s, he became mayor of Williamsburg in 1766 and accumulated the financial means to own nineteen slaves. The house where the widower Everard resided with his daughters (both of whom would marry well) was a manifestation of his elevated status. When Everard sold his previous house on Nicholson Street and moved to Palace Green, the move symbolized his ascension to membership in the privileged class known as the gentry.

The house had been built by a gunsmith, John Brush, in 1718. It was not large by later standards, standing one-story tall and one-room deep. But the symmetrical facade of the house bespoke an evident aspiration, with modillions decorating its cornice and double-hung sash windows. Brush almost immediately added two wings to the rear, but during the decade of his ownership he left the interior of the house partially unfinished. Its completion was left to Henry Cary Jr., a builder who after 1729 added cornices, chair boards, and baseboards to the two principal rooms, the parlor and dining room. The skilled Cary, who had worked on some of the finest buildings in town, including the Governor's Palace and the President's House at the College of William and Mary, introduced a sophisticated staircase into his own house. He located it in the central passage (hallway), which until that date had lacked even plaster on its walls (access to the upper floor was by a temporary staircase or a ladder). He put down new flooring and painted the trim Spanish brown, made from red lead and Spanish brown pigment.

By the time Everard purchased the house in 1756, he had already become deputy clerk of the York County Court. Within a few years his list of offices also included mayor of Williamsburg, vestryman at Bruton Parish Church, founding trustee of the Public Hospital, and committee clerk at the House of Burgesses. He took to riding around town in a coach driven by slaves in livery. His public prominence gave him new social standing, and consistent with his power and prestige, a genteel domicile was required. It had become time to outfit his house anew.

In the early 1770s, he updated his home in a stylish manner to impress his friends and neighbors. The wainscot and chimneypieces he added to the parlor and dining room, together with Cary's earlier staircase, meant the assembled interior woodwork was among the finest in Williamsburg. As finely crafted as the woodwork was, however, Everard chose to use color to communicate his taste and sophistication. When the time came to restore the house, first in 1949–51 and again in the 1990s, the Thomas Everard House proved to be the repository of some surprising evidence of its own past. Beneath the roof of the north wing, remnants were found of the original riven (split) clapboard roof surface. The original south wing was long

FACING PAGE: The dormers probably came later, but from the front, this still very much resembles the house that John Brush built in 1718. Paint analysis revealed that the exterior was originally painted a reddish brown ("Spanish brown"), but like most of the houses in Williamsburg, by the third quarter of the eighteenth century it had been painted white.

gone, but archaeology on the site made it possible to reconstruct it. Investigation established that the central passage was original to the 1718 construction date, making it one of the first such spaces in colonial Virginia. But it was an extensive paint analysis that enabled the house to be restored to Everard's updating in 1770. What draws the eye now—and would have been admired by Everard's guests—are the finishes on the walls. The dining room and rear chamber have reproduction wallpapers in patterns based on paper fragments found during the initial restoration of the house after

Colonial Williamsburg acquired the property. The principal room, the parlor, was not papered—its plaster was and is whitewashed—but its woodwork was painted and glazed. In Everard's time, candlelight would have endowed the rich green hue with an almost luminescent effect.

Everard had chosen a nicely detailed house of modest size in a prideful location, as close as any other dwelling to the most powerful presence in the colony, the royal governor. During his ownership, he raised its appearance to a higher status, one commensurate with his own. ◠

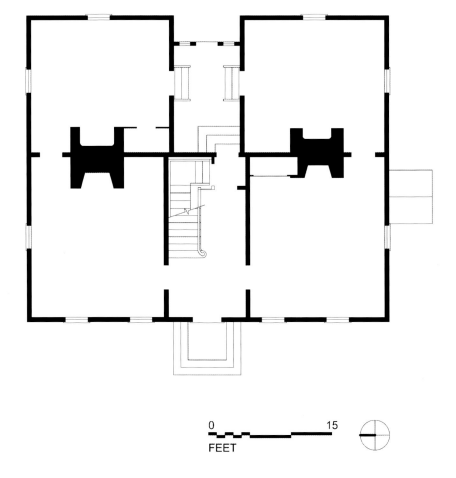

The house has a U-shape plan. The parlor, dining room, and central passage at the front date from the initial construction phase in 1718–19, while the north wing with its bedchamber to the rear was added about 1720. The south wing is a twentieth-century reconstruction of a structure that in Everard's time likely contained his study.

0   15
FEET

The house before restoration, with a later porch and large, protruding center dormer

TOP, LEFT: A dormer gains surprising elegance thanks to the molded pediment that caps it.

TOP, RIGHT: Though Brush built himself a small house—the original footprint was only forty-four feet wide and twenty deep—he finished it with some high-style details, including a modillioned cornice that not so many years later would be de rigueur in large Georgian-style dwellings.

BOTTOM, LEFT: The work of a blacksmith, a Suffolk latch like this one was a rarity in early Williamsburg homes.

BOTTOM, RIGHT: The front entrance to the house features few elaborations, but the door and its eight raised panels nevertheless speak for the craft of the joiner who made them.

The outbuildings at the rear of the property. The building at left served as the kitchen— one of only a few extant eighteenth-century examples left in town—while the smaller building served as a smokehouse.

The brilliant green in the parlor has been likened to the green of a lollipop; certainly, it seems to shimmer. The astonishingly bright color was achieved by applying a layer of green paint and several layers of a glaze pigmented with verdigris (copper acetate, a precipitate prepared by applying vinegar to sheet copper).

The staircase that Henry Cary Jr. installed was lined with raised panel wainscot and its treads decorated with carved brackets—features more characteristic of larger and more imposing planters' homes. Cary knew about such up-market construction, having built the President's House at the College of William and Mary.

Fronted by a picket fence, the small structure at right is a reconstruction of a lost building that served as an office.

George Wythe House

PALACE GREEN STREET

CONSTRUCTED 1752–54

Both the man and the house that bears his name are central to the Williamsburg story. George Wythe (pronounced to rhyme with Smith) was an influential lawyer and legislator before and after the revolution, as well as a signer of the Declaration of Independence. He was a teacher, too, and among his star pupils were Thomas Jefferson (who described Wythe as "my faithful Mentor in youth, and my most affectionate friend through life"); and John Marshall who, as chief justice, would play a crucial part in defining the Supreme Court's authority in the early years of the nineteenth century.

While Wythe left his imprint on the home, the impressive brick house never actually belonged to him. It was constructed in the early 1750s by Richard Taliaferro, a planter and sometime undertaker (in the eighteenth-century sense, that is, meaning contractor). He may have built the house on speculation, but when his daughter, Elizabeth, married George Wythe in 1755, Taliaferro granted them life tenancy. George Wythe would remain in residence for thirty-six years, until his departure for Richmond to assume a judgeship in 1791 (Elizabeth had died in 1787).

In Wythe's time, his home was regarded as the finest private dwelling in town, and that perception survives today, since buyers of the Colonial Williamsburg line of house plans have made the Wythe house the top seller by far. Part of the explanation for its appeal then and now is that unlike most of the earlier houses in Williamsburg, this house was conceived as a whole. It was not a product of a series of building campaigns. Rather than being the end result of an evolutionary process that added wings or dormers, this balanced, symmetrical, and boldly proportioned house was designed of-a-piece. The two-story Wythe house would be described today in realtor talk as a "classic colonial." In architectural terms, however, it is more precisely classified as a five-bay, double-pile house (meaning there are five vertical sets of openings across its facade and that the plan is two rooms deep). When the Wythe house was constructed in the 1750s, it represented an important new precedent. Earlier houses in Williamsburg typically had consisted of only two or three rooms on the main floor, plus an entrance hall or passage (one example is the Nelson-Galt House, see page 18). Such plans had evolved to meet changing needs and tastes. In contrast, the Wythe house signaled a shift from the local by adopting a more cosmopolitan model that flaunted the wealth and importance of the residents.

The rectangular footprint of the Wythe house allowed for four rooms to be symmetrically arranged on each floor. Upon being welcomed to the house, the visitor enters a spacious passage that, as in earlier houses, opens to a parlor on one side and a dining room on the other, which, in turn, opens to a bedchamber. The passage also allowed

FACING PAGE: The house is distinctly formal, with its precise symmetry. It is a carefully calculated mathematical arrangement composed to loom large and important. The hip roof adds to its imposing presence, as do the massive chimneys. Note, too, that the windows are smaller on the second floor than the first, which serves to emphasize the presence of the house on the streetscape.

access to a second room in the rear. For lawyer, jurist, and teacher George Wythe, that space became the study where he tutored Jefferson; in other Virginia examples, this added first-floor room served as a nursery, bedchamber, or informal dining parlor. The staircase had become a grand statement, too, leading to four upper bedchambers that, like the rooms on the first floor, flanked the stair passage in symmetrical pairs.

After the Wythe tenancy, later owners of the house made changes. A large wooden portico was added to the front about 1800; a half century after that, a Victorian-era porch replaced it. Inside, wainscot and new mantels were added, as was a kitchen and pantry. In the twentieth century, the house again became home to an important player in Williamsburg, Dr. W. A. R. Goodwin, who

TOP: From the southeast, the two-story house towers over Palace Green yet has an air of reserve, perhaps even of restrained dignity.

BOTTOM: This was the first dwelling in town in which the shape of the house was its most evident characteristic. The mass of the house expresses its importance, its weight, its significance; the surface details are understated.

conceived the restoration at Williamsburg. In 1927 he moved into the Wythe house, which had been adapted for use as Bruton Parish Church's parish house. In 1939–40, Colonial Williamsburg embarked upon its first restoration of the house.

The vast majority of building fabric is original. For the most part, the brick superstructure, the frame, the windows, doors, hardware, and the floors date from Wythe's time. The decorative finishes inside still posed challenges to restorers, and only in the last decade of the twentieth century was Wythe's decorative scheme installed. Among other changes, appropriate mantels were reinserted, but it was the addition of wallpapers that transformed the look of the house.

Paint analysis suggested that most of the woodwork had been repainted about 1770 in a soft ocher (yellow), a color often used in combination with papers. While no original wallpaper survived from the Wythe era, an array of wallpaper patterns appropriate to Wythe's known uses of the rooms was identified and reproduced. For visitors today who expect trim painted in muted colors and plain plastered walls, the brilliant colors and bold patterns of these papers can be shocking. In their own time, they were a revelation—only a generation before, a coat of Spanish brown was the standard paint scheme. But in the years preceding the revolution, wallpaper became fashionable and indeed appropriate to the high station of men such as Wythe and even George Washington, who used this house as his headquarters before the decisive battle at nearby Yorktown in 1781. ◭

TOP AND MIDDLE: The masons who constructed the house added subtle architectural interest to it by using rubbed bricks to emphasize the windows, including those to the basement and over the entrance. Bricks chosen carefully for their uniform color were abraded against a stone or other bricks; the rubbed surfaces, being smoother and more consistent in color, draw attention to details such as the string course across the front of the house and the quoin-like bricks laid on each side of the transom window. The rubbed and gauged (wedge-shaped) bricks were used to form the flattened arches over the openings and, together with thin mortar joints, also help articulate details.

BOTTOM: The front steps were reconstructed based on evidence found of the shape and location in the front wall of the house. After leaving Williamsburg in 1791 to serve on Virginia's Court of Chancery, Wythe resided in Richmond. He died of unnatural causes fifteen years later; his grandnephew, George Wythe Sweeney, was suspected but never convicted of poisoning Wythe.

FACING PAGE: The fine
staircase in the passage, its
balustrade one of the few
unpainted surfaces in the
house. It was likely finished
only with a coating of wax.
The open doorway over-
looks the green lined with
topiary.

In the 1770s, the woodwork
in all but two of the rooms
was repainted. The color
here in the dining room
became a pale yellow ocher,
with chocolate baseboards,
mantel, and doors. Thus, it
was the "wall hangings"
(wallpaper) that gave the
rooms individual distinction.

The first-floor bedchamber is at the rear of the house, immediately behind the dining room. Later owners added an exterior door and converted the space into an "inner kitchen."

FACING PAGE: Though all signs of the original papers had been removed from the master chamber before the house's restoration, the restorers developed a decorative scheme using a range of evidence, including surviving fragments at the nearby Thomas Everard House and Robert Carter's purchase orders for his dwelling just north on Palace Green.

TOP: The Georgian plan of the house rationalized the growing needs of the gentry. Its plan was more regular—the house became one uniform box, with a symmetrical arrangement of rooms.

BOTTOM: Wythe's house as updated for Goodwin, ca. 1930. Note the split-pediment colonial revival frontispiece.

FACING PAGE: At the rear of the house Wythe was able to enjoy his pleasure garden, but just behind the shrubbery was a virtual village of support buildings where the Wythes' slaves (they had between fifteen and twenty) worked. Among the structures were a smokehouse, kitchen, poultry house and dovecote, and stable.

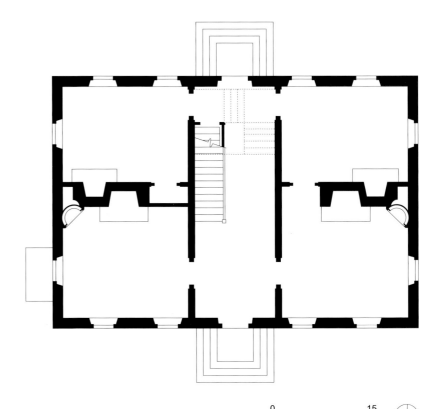

0   15
FEET

Tayloe House

This was the modest, in-town house of a man of immodest means. Colonel John Tayloe II owned a profitable ironworks in Alexandria. He built one of colonial Virginia's finest mansions, Mount Airy, on his plantation some seventy-five miles north of Williamsburg on the Rappahannock River (in which Tayloe descendants still reside). He was a member of the Governor's Council, the upper legislative body in Virginia and, when in Williamsburg, he required suitable accommodations and a place to entertain his influential guests.

The house he purchased in 1759 had been built for Dr. James Carter, physician at the College of William and Mary and proprietor of an apothecary on Duke of Gloucester Street called the Unicorn's Horn. Carter had purchased the property in 1752 for £200, but his improvements—which included the house, probably built about 1757—enabled him to sell it to Tayloe for £600.

The location was a desirable one, close to Palace Green; the house, though not large, was substantial for its time. The roof enclosed a full second story, as well as a tall attic with two more rooms. Generous windows allowed ample light to enter but, ironically, also made the exterior seem smaller than it was, belying the fact that within its walls were eight rooms, some of which were finished with very stylish paneling and other woodwork.

The interior layout, like that at the William Lightfoot House (see page 106), is a "side-passage" floor plan. The front and rear entrances open into what today would be called a hall that runs the full depth of the house along its eastern gable end. This first-floor passage contained stairs to the second floor, as well as doorways on the interior wall that led to the parlor at the front of the house and to the dining room at the rear. The passages upstairs and down would have been used as added living spaces, particularly in warm weather when the ventilation provided by the multiple openings would have welcomed cooling breezes. Like other homes of the gentry in eighteenth-century Williamsburg, the Tayloe House had purpose-built outbuildings, including a kitchen, laundry, smokehouse, storehouse, stable, and privy. Several original buildings survive, among them an elegant office. The latter is prominently placed, its front facade aligned on the streetscape with the house with an ogee-shaped roof that is unique in Williamsburg.

Restored in 1950–51, today the Tayloe House is not open to the public but is a private residence. The rear porch has been converted to a kitchen and the house has two bathrooms. In a sense, then, it remains in disguise, a house with an exterior that belies what is inside. ◭

FACING PAGE: The deceptively humble front facade of the Tayloe House on Nicholson Street

PAGES 56–57: When Colonial Williamsburg acquired the house in 1950, it came complete with a two-story addition, which had been constructed in the nineteenth century. It was subsequently removed, returning the streetscape to its eighteenth-century appearance, with the house and Tayloe Office standing a discrete distance apart.

TOP, LEFT: The dormer stands farther away from the roof at its peak but flush at the sill. The effect inside is less the shaft of light characteristic of dormers than a generalized illumination typical of windows in traditional walls.

TOP, RIGHT: One of the distinguishing characteristics of the house is its double-pitched roof. Note the unusual "kick," or flare, at the eaves.

BOTTOM: The side-passage plan was an efficient one, with each of the four major rooms (two on the first floor, two above) being served by corner fireplaces constructed in a single chimney mass. The first and second floors are virtually identical in plan.

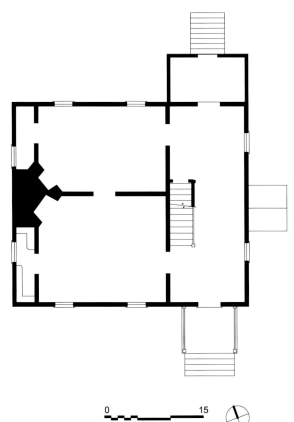

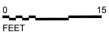

0   15
FEET

TOP: The Tayloe Office is in the foreground, the reconstructed kitchen just beyond. The distinctive office, which probably dates from the late eighteenth century, is approximately 15½-feet square. Observe the grace note—the finial at the peak of the ogee-shaped roof.

BOTTOM: During the office's restoration in 1937, the building's skin was removed to reveal its framing. The roof in particular, with its multiple radii and miters, is an artful display of the framer's craft.

Ludwell-Paradise House

DUKE OF GLOUCESTER STREET
CONSTRUCTED CA. 1752–55

For Rent: a "Very Good Dwelling-House." And there's more: owner Philip Ludwell III was offering not just a new house but also its privy, garden, stable, and coach house as well. The advertisement, placed in the Williamsburg newspaper, the *Virginia Gazette*, soon attracted a tenant.

The setting was desirable, as the location was "on the main street, lower Side of the Market Place." The house itself was impressive, very stylish when Ludwell placed his advertisement in 1755, and a series of renters leased the place for the balance of the eighteenth century. For a time it was a fashionable tavern, a place the royal governor chose to entertain "some of the principal Gentlemen of the city." Colonel George Washington found accommodations there, too, as a young man fresh from his military service in the French and Indian War, who had come to Williamsburg to serve in the Virginia House of Burgesses. From the 1760s until October of 1775, the house was home to the very newspaper that carried the original ad, the *Gazette*, which was printed on the premises for almost a decade.

The Ludwell-Paradise House has the appearance of a classic colonial, five-bays wide with a center entrance like the George Wythe House (see page 44). It has similar details, with a hip roof, a chimney at each end, and fine brickwork. Unlike the Wythe house, the main block is only one room deep, with a one-story shed across the back.

After the revolution, the house continued to have its share of intriguing residents and guests. One was Lucy Paradise, Ludwell's second daughter, who resided there for many years. She became a well-known Williamsburg eccentric and ended her life in residence at Williamsburg's Public Hospital, the first public institution in America to provide for "idiots, lunatics, and other persons of unsound Minds." The Marquis de Lafayette dined at the Ludwell-Paradise House when he visited Williamsburg on his 1824 American tour, but it was another iconic personage who, a century later, would turn the calendar back to the time of Philip Ludwell. Today's Colonial Williamsburg formally began in 1926 when John D. Rockefeller Jr. secretly purchased this, his first Williamsburg house (his identity was shielded, as the telegram sent Dr. Goodwin to authorize the purchase of the "antique" was signed simply "David's father").

The house was converted to gallery spaces during the early days of Colonial Williamsburg, and Abby Aldrich Rockefeller's folk art collection was exhibited there until 1957. Truly an adaptable building, the Ludwell-Paradise House could count among its incarnations a tavern, office, and museum before its restoration to its original use in 1959. Today, it is again rented as a private residence, its reserved eighteenth-century face helping to define the restored streetscape of Duke of Gloucester Street. ⚜

FACING PAGE: A grand, imposing house when completed in the mid-1750s, its prideful facade towers, cliff-like, over the sidewalk lining the north side of Duke of Gloucester Street.

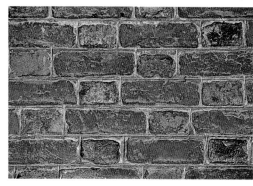

TOP, LEFT AND RIGHT: The ca. 1920 remodeling had involved a new front doorway with a pedimented cap. That was removed, and the eighteenth-century-style transom put in its place. In the same way, two-over-two Victorian replacement windows were removed, and appropriate nine-over-nine sash installed. The openings in the brick had also been changed, so the restorers raised them once again to their original height.

BOTTOM, LEFT: The original appearance of the window grilles admitting air to the full basement was also restored in 1931.

BOTTOM, RIGHT: The masonry adds richness to the surface of the structure. Laid in "Flemish bond," meaning the brickwork consists of courses in which brick ends (headers) are alternated with bricks laid lengthwise (stretchers). Here, the Flemish bond is given an added accent by the use of glazed headers.

FACING PAGE: The masonry work endows the house with much of its character, thanks to the horizontal belt-course across the facade, the pattern of the brickwork itself, and the bricklike hues of the painted trim.

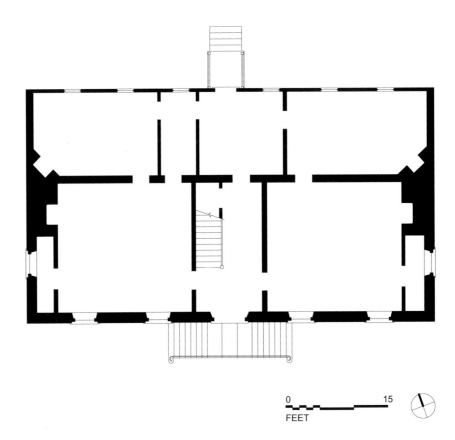

0   15

FEET

TOP: The main block of the house was one-room deep, but the lean-to structure at the rear provided added first-floor space.

BOTTOM: A 1920s renovation had transformed the Ludwell-Paradise House, so the 1931 restoration required that the porch be removed to return the house to its prerevolutionary appearance.

FACING PAGE: Though some observers hypothesized that the shedlike structure to the rear of the two-story main block was a later addition, a close examination of the brickwork led architectural historians to conclude the entire structure was built in one campaign in the early 1750s.

Robert Carter House

In the early eighteenth century, a few Virginia families acquired such wealth and power that they assumed the status of dynasties. Perhaps none of their patriarchs wielded more influence than Robert "King" Carter who, at his death in 1732, owned approximately three-hundred-thousand acres and one thousand slaves. He had served as treasurer for the Virginia colony, speaker of its House of Burgesses, and president of the Governor's Council. This Williamsburg house bears the name of one of his principal heirs.

When Robert Carter III took up residence in 1761, the house had stood for perhaps a dozen years. For whom and when it had been constructed is not clear, though an apothecary, Dr. Kenneth McKenzie, owned the house and operated his shop on the property prior to 1751 (the McKenzie Apothecary has been reconstructed and is in operation as McKenzie's Store today). That the home even then was large and commodious is certain, since it served as temporary quarters for the royal governor, Robert Dinwiddie, while the Governor's Palace was being renovated in 1751–52. The house changed ownership several times before Robert Carter III purchased the property in 1761 for £650, then a princely sum. And he invested more funds in adapting the house to his social station and education (he had been sent to England where he studied at the Inns of Court). Like his grandfather, he, too,

played a prominent political role in colonial Virginia, serving seventeen years in the upper body of the legislature, the Governor's Council, having been appointed to one of its twelve seats by the king's ministers.

When seen at a distance, the Carter house is large and imposing by the standards of eighteenth-century Williamsburg. Built on a footprint almost forty-six-feet wide and thirty deep, the two-story house easily is distinguished by its double-hip roof. Unlike a simple hip roof, in which the ridge of the familiar gable shape is shortened at each end to form triangular roof surfaces, a double-hip roof has a second hip with a flatter pitch that crowns the lower hip. In the Carter house, the upper hip was added by Carter to enclose an earlier set of ridges and valleys. That "M-roof" caught rainwater, which flowed back outside via internal gutters. Dormers added at both ends provided light and ventilation, making the attic habitable.

This is a house with two faces—the main facade has fewer windows than the rear and is flanked by several buildings that effectively screen the generous garden behind the home. This was not a dwelling that welcomed all comers: On the contrary, even the floor plan suggests a desire to winnow out visitors of lesser station. Arrivals were admitted first into the passage, an L-shape entrance hall that functioned as a public waiting room for servants and guests. Genteel visitors might be admitted to a front parlor that opened

FACING PAGE: The plain, three-bay front facade hardly reflected the wealth and power of the Carter family.

PAGES 68–69: The house and its dependencies (a shop, left, and an office, right) were built on a double lot. The great length of the combined buildings effectively screened the gardens to the rear.

directly off the passage, but only the privileged few would have been invited to the largest and best appointed room in the house, the dining room to the rear. The opportunity to dine with the Carters was the ultimate compliment to a visitor, who might also be invited to take a turn in the ornamental gardens to the rear. The terraced contours of this private landscape are still apparent.

The house had many new appointments in the Carter years. The family added fashionable wallpapers and upgraded the floors and even the doors, adding mortise locks, a fashionable contrivance of the period. Yet by 1772 it seemed "not sufficiently roomy." Since the prospects were for a still larger family (when they departed Williamsburg, Robert and his wife, Frances, were accompanied by six of the eventual seventeen children she would bear him), the Carters removed permanently to their plantation, Nomini Hall, in Westmoreland County.

In the years that followed, its ownership changed and the house was subject to other renovation schemes. An early-nineteenth-century owner, Robert Saunders, added a porch across the rear that served to connect the garden more directly to the living space of the house. A few decades later, a two-story Grecian portico was added to the front facade, resulting in a reorientation of living patterns in the house. In the manner of the era, the residents probably spent a good deal of time on its upper level, this time at the front, regarding the streetscape.

In 1928 the Carter house was purchased by the Reverend W. A. R. Goodwin on behalf of John D. Rockefeller Jr. The first restoration took place in 1931–32, when the Grecian portico was removed along with many other later accretions, including the attic dormers. What has emerged from the ongoing study and restoration of the Carter house is a grand home for a scion of one of Virginia's first families. Its site gave it prominence—it is at the right hand of the Governor's Palace—and its generous proportions, gardens, and flanking colonnades enhance that sense of power and wealth. Today it is an element of the streetscape, not a museum house open to the public but a blind face behind which there are offices and meeting rooms. ◍

The house's first-floor plan is unique in Williamsburg, with its L-shaped hall, which opens to the parlor. The rear passage led to a bedchamber to the left and the largest and finest room in the house, the dining room, to the right.

0   15
FEET

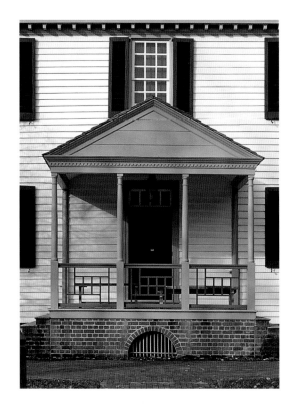

TOP, LEFT: Since the original porch was gone, the restorers modeled the reconstructed entrance portico on one at Tuckahoe, an early Virginia manse where Thomas Jefferson spent much of his childhood.

TOP, RIGHT: The entrance portico and the reconstructed north colonnade and office beyond it

BOTTOM: The front door and bold transom light

When constructed, this archway with its keystone and bold molding conveyed to visitors more than the good taste and wealth of the householder. It was also a portal, leading from the passage (reception hall) to the dining room and a master chamber (bedroom) to the rear. Those who were invited to pass were privileged; all but a few were excluded.

FACING PAGE: In the eighteenth century, staircases offered the joiner an opportunity to show off, and the man who crafted this one took full advantage, incorporating raised-panel wainscot, three turned balusters per tread, and a beaded and paneled newel. The stairs date to the original construction of the house in the late 1740s.

TOP: The original cornice was removed, probably in one of the nineteenth-century renovations. The cornice on the house today, with its ornamental modillion blocks, was fabricated to resemble what seems to have been a standard form in the mid-eighteenth century. It was based on surviving cornices on the Peyton Randolph, Ludwell-Paradise, and other Williamsburg houses.

BOTTOM: During the nineteenth century, a broad, two-story Greek Revival entrance portico was added.

TOP AND BOTTOM: There is a striking difference between the front (top) and rear elevations of the house. The former has three sets of openings, while the other has five. A rarity in eighteenth-century architecture, this change in fenestration from one facade to another reflects the private and public faces of the house.

James Geddy House

James Geddy Jr. was a harbinger. He was not a member of the landed gentry; he was not a Virginia lawyer or clerk whose training helped him shape a career in politics. Despite being the son of a tradesman, he aspired to the status of gentleman and, in some measure, achieved his goal. The home he built for himself reflected his ambitions and those of countless others who aspired to climb the social ladder.

In August of 1760 he purchased for £100 a "Peice [sic] Parcel or Lot of Land with [its] Appurtenances" from his widowed mother. His father, a gunsmith, had constructed a house and forge on the premises some twenty years earlier, but the son was not satisfied with his parents' "appurtenances." He demolished the earlier structure and proceeded to build his own two-story house on much the same site. Geddy the younger had learned his father's trade and more, becoming a silversmith and an entrepreneur. He catered to a prosperous clientele and, in the years to come, sought to join their ranks. He would soon own more than a dozen slaves, hold minor public offices, and eventually sell his holdings in Williamsburg and move westward to Petersburg, Virginia, where he lived until his death in 1807. But it was in Williamsburg that Geddy quite literally raised the visibility and prominence of his family.

When viewed from the street, the main block of the house of James Geddy Jr. has two substantial faces overlooking Palace Green Street and Duke of Gloucester Street from its corner lot. The tall expanse of the three-bay elevations suggests a large and generous house, but that is partly illusory, as the floor plan in not square at all but L-shaped, containing just three rooms and a passage on the first floor. Yet the house dominates its site, an effect that is enhanced by the two shops in an attached wing that extends along Williamsburg's principal commercial way, Duke of Gloucester Street. One of those storefronts was probably the shop from which Geddy's own goods were sold, the other an income property rented to commercial tenants.

Just as Peyton Randolph had done when he updated his home a half-dozen years earlier (see page 26), Geddy made the dining room the most elegant space in his house. Not only was it the largest room, but it also had the most expensive floor joinery of the age and its walls probably were papered. Wallpaper had become the height of fashion by the 1760s, and Geddy's guests would have recognized its presence as an expression of his wealth and newfound status. Geddy's house is not an artful design. The house looks bulky, the roof compressed. While the finishes inside (the wallpapers and paneling, for example) and outside (a modillioned cornice and portico) reflect Geddy's aspirations, this house was plain indeed when compared with the stylish dwellings of the wealthiest merchants and planters in the colonies. Even its shape suggests a good deal about the

FACING PAGE: Seen from the south, the Geddy shop (right) adjoins the main block of the house.

The decorated portico is a rich source of decorative ideas, featuring turned balusters on its upper railing and a modillioned cornice (top, left); raised plinths beneath fluted columns (top, right); and a delicate iron railing across the stoop. The portico today, in fact, is probably more elaborate than the original, as it is a twentieth-century reconstruction based on a mix of physical and archaeological evidence.

FACING PAGE: The plainer face of tradesman Geddy's house overlooks Palace Green Street.

TOP: The house before restoration; on the exterior, little changed

BOTTOM: The floor plan reflects the elements that had become standard in colonial Virginia by the time James Geddy Jr. built this house. From the front door on Duke of Gloucester Street, the visitor would enter the passage. The passage contained the stairs to the chambers above and three doors to the principal rooms on the main floor, which included a parlor, dining room, and chamber. The latter probably was used for sleeping and as an administrative center, or counting room, for Geddy's adjoining shop.

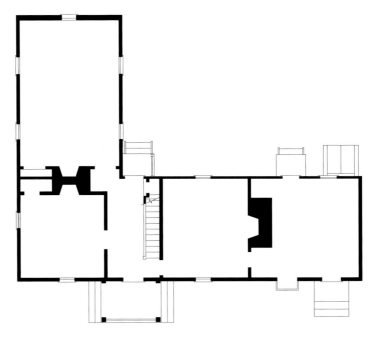

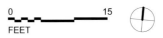

0   15
FEET

house: the building effectively screens off much of its rear yard and Geddy's manufactory with its forge and unsightly collection of supplies and refuse. Burned ash, slag, and wood for the forge fire are still to be seen today, as the Geddy house is an exhibition site, with interpreters manning the foundry and shop.

No doubt Geddy saw his new house as good for business: he acknowledged that the site of his shop was perhaps "too high up Town" (that is, far from the bustle of the Capitol), but by building a bigger and grander place than his father had done, he sought to enhance his own standing. He launched himself, selling high-grade goods of his making in cast bronze, brass, and pewter, as well as items imported from England. But to the discerning eye, there was no mistaking that this was the house of a striving tradesman, not the sophisticated dwelling of a man of refinement. ◑

The Palace Green Street side of the house with its dependencies visible at the rear

Coke-Garrett House

NICHOLSON STREET

CONSTRUCTED CA. 1755–62

ADDITIONS CONSTRUCTED ABOUT 1810, 1836–37, AND IN THE 1850S

This is a crazy quilt of a house. Unlike so many other homes in Colonial Williamsburg, the Coke-Garrett House has not had its calendar turned back to the eighteenth century but retains generations of nineteenth-century changes. Though it is not an exhibition house (the president of The Colonial Williamsburg Foundation resides here), even seen from the street it is a visual essay on a century of American architectural evolution.

The earliest portion of the house was built somewhere between 1755 and 1762 by a tavern keeper and goldsmith named John Coke. He used timbers recycled from an earlier structure to build a story-and-a-half house in keeping with the taste of his times. Its pre-revolutionary appearance consisted of a center entrance that led to a passage with a parlor to one side and a chamber on the other.

A half-century later, Richard Garrett renovated the house in a more up-to-date style. He replaced the old-fashioned Coke-era finishes about 1810, installing new windows and trim on the outside, along with replacement doors and mantels inside, and new Chinese lattice railings on a stairway and the portico. But Garrett was not finished. About the same time, he added a freestanding building to the east of the house. Constructed as an office some forty feet away, its roof ridge was raised perpendicular to the house's, enabling its facade to be given a temple front with four freestanding columns and overhanging pediment. It is a proud and pretty building constructed of bricks salvaged from an earlier building that had burned on the same site.

Richard Garrett's son, Robert, also took his turn at remodeling the house when, in 1836–37, he grafted a new two-story, four-bay wing to the house. The addition enclosed a new passage at the east end of the structure, as well as generous first-floor parlor and bedchambers above on the second and attic floors. Finally, in the 1850s, the remaining space between Robert Garrett's addition and the office his father had built was infilled with a smaller late-eighteenth or early-nineteenth-century structure moved from an unknown site.

As a result of these extensive changes and additions, the Coke-Garrett House posed an intriguing set of challenges when, in 1928, the attempt to return the town to its eighteenth-century appearance was just beginning. The house came complete with a life tenant, a descendant named Miss Lottie Garrett from whom Dr. Goodwin had purchased the property. The restorers installed paneling salvaged from another house—a practice long since discontinued—and planted an elaborate formal garden. Much later a modern kitchen was introduced into the brick office.

Since the ca. 1810 renovation had left few surfaces untouched, the Coke-Garrett House proved an unsuitable candidate for restoration to its eighteenth-century appearance. Yet the house as it stands today— stately, commodious, handsomely situated a comfortable distance from Nicholson Street—reflects as few other Williamsburg structures do the architectural advances that prosperous owners such as the Garretts incorporated in the decades before the Civil War. ◭

FACING PAGE: The south front of the Coke-Garrett House consisting of four distinguishable parts (left to right): the original house, constructed 1755–62; the 1836–37 addition; the ca. 1800 section moved to the site in the 1850s; and the ca. 1810 office.

TOP, LEFT: The office, added about 1810, has served many purposes, including as a surgery for Dr. Robert M. Garrett during the Civil War, where he treated Union and Confederate soldiers after the Battle of Williamsburg. In 1971, it was converted to a modern kitchen.

TOP, RIGHT, AND BOTTOM: The entrance portico here is a rarity. Much admired in their time, few Chinese Chippendale porch railings survive though they have had an enduring popularity and have been often imitated in recent years. This one dates from ca. 1810.

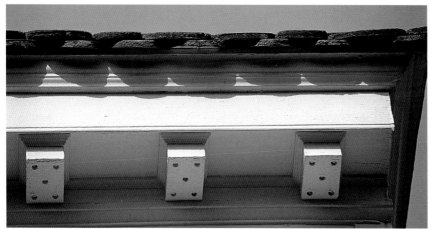

TOP, LEFT: Overlooking the streetscapes of Williamsburg are a range of dormers that add charm—as well as light—to the houses' second stories. This is an 1830s version of Williamsburg's ever-popular pedimented dormer.

TOP, RIGHT: The shaped endboard is the result of the twentieth-century restoration, but portions of the cornice survive from the mid-eigteenth century.

BOTTOM: The modillion blocks on the two-story portion of the house date from the 1836–37 renovation.

TOP: Despite its disparate elements, the house has a rich dignity. The same was true in 1935, when the porch on the tall central section and the formal colonial revival gardens were in place, as this photograph taken by F. S. Lincoln for *Architectural Record* demonstrates.

BOTTOM: The result of the house's multiple building campaigns and restorations is a hodgepodge of periods and plans. There are two front-to-back passages, two parlors, and an office that has become a kitchen—but somehow it all works.

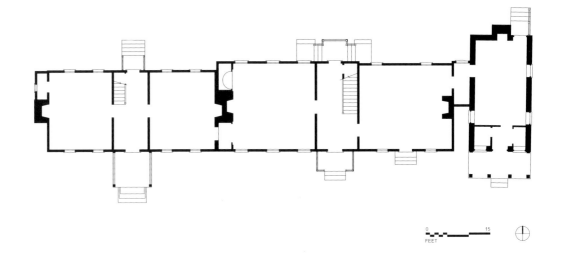

0   15
FEET

The elegant simplicity of Coke's dwelling, the west-ernmost of the four sections of the house, was popular in its own time (note the obvi-ous resemblance to some of its contemporaries, among them the Nelson-Galt and Thomas Everard houses; see pages 18 and 36). Such one-story, five-bay houses were found up and down the coast (the Cape Cod house in the Northeast is a distant relation) and have been built in large numbers ever since.

Benjamin Powell House

WALLER STREET

CONSTRUCTED BEFORE 1763; FRONT WING ADDED BEFORE 1782

Waller Street was at the edge of town when Benjamin Powell acquired this property in 1763. The people who were buying lots and building homes east of the Capitol and Public Gaol were tradesmen making their way in the world, and Powell, a house carpenter and joiner, could count among his neighbors two bricklayers, a cabinetmaker, harness maker, bookbinder, tailor, and butcher. Even if the area lacked the prestige of Palace Green or the commercial buzz of Duke of Gloucester Street, it had the character of a neighborhood.

Powell was something of a wheeler-dealer buying, improving, and then reselling a number of nearby lots, but he chose to reside for almost twenty years at this address. At the time he purchased it, a substantial brick house probably stood on the property. The dwelling consisted of three downstairs rooms (a hall or parlor; a kitchen; and a chamber) as well as a habitable space above reached from the hall by an enclosed stair. A smaller, one-story wing attached to the east contained a service space, perhaps a laundry. But Powell wanted more, so he constructed a wood-frame addition, incorporating the original brick structure as a rear wing.

The result was a much grander house. The new section at the front was arranged like many other houses of the time around a central passage (hallway) with a parlor on one side and a bedchamber on the other. The passage also featured a handsome new staircase and opened at the rear to the original brick structure where the partition between an old chamber and hall had been removed to make them into a single space. This spacious dining room became the focus of Powell's house, while the kitchen and service wing behind remained much as before.

The Benjamin Powell dwelling is an exhibition house today but one with a difference. Unlike most of the other homes at Colonial Williamsburg that are open to the public, the Powell House is not packed with historic furniture. That means that climate control is not essential, so the windows are opened on warm days. School groups who visit find hands-on activities in the Powell house. The effect is open and relaxed. In the eighteenth century the central passage in many homes became summer living areas, so the Powell house passage has Windsor chairs of the sort that would have been used not only inside but outdoors, too. While still a museum space, the house feels more natural, with a flow of people and breezes such as it might have had in the eighteenth century.

Benjamin Powell became one of one of the most successful carpenters of his generation in Williamsburg, working on the Public Gaol, adding the steeple to Bruton Parish Church, and as undertaker (general contractor) for the building of the Public Hospital. His success enabled him to buy a substantial property (some 220 acres) out of town, a "plantation" to which he retired after the Revolutionary War. By the time he sold this house in 1782, the successful tradesmen had elevated himself in the world and had taken to adding the word "Gent." to his signature. 🪭

FACING PAGE: The house that Benjamin Powell built: the new face he added gave it a proud countenance overlooking Waller Street.

TOP AND FACING PAGE:
After Powell sold it, the
house saw its share of
changes, among them the
addition of a full-height
second story and a two-
story porch. Once the
nineteenth-century addi-
tions had been removed
in the 1950s restoration,
the house regained its
eighteenth-century scale.

BOTTOM: The L-shaped
floor plan resulted when
Powell added the three-
room structure across the
front to the earlier brick
building.

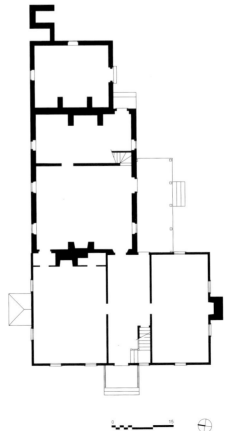

0   15
FEET

FACING PAGE: Symmetry was not—and is not—a hard and fast rule: note the varied spacing of the windows in the facade of Powell's addition. Yet it still retains its distinguished air.

Though within the walls of the earlier house, this room was the result of Powell's renovation in which he removed a central partition (note the boxed beam on the ceiling, indicating the onetime position of the wall) that divided the earlier chamber and hall. The result was a dining room that, in its time, was one of Williamsburg's largest and most impressive, complete with raised-panel wainscot and an imposing chimney breast that reaches the ceiling.

The first-floor chamber where Benjamin and Annabelle Powell slept would also have been her office, the place from which she administered the affairs of the house. Despite its curtained bedstead, this chamber had less elaborate appointments than the public spaces in the house.

FACING PAGE: Houses that evolve over time, as this one did, sometimes have a charming eccentricity. Here, at the rear of the original brick dwelling, is an attached one-story scullery or laundry; inside was a large fireplace, its six-foot-plus width well suited to the work of washing.

Palmer House

DUKE OF GLOUCESTER STREET
CONSTRUCTED CA. 1754

The site was prominent: the Palmer House is the dwelling on Duke of Gloucester Street that is closest to the Capitol. It was built of brick, a material that in itself implied wealth and permanence. That is not to say, however, that the house has remained unchanged over the last 250 years.

John Palmer was a lawyer who became the bursar of the College of William and Mary. He had acquired the property in 1749, but the house that stands today was constructed after a 1754 fire destroyed the "well-finished Brick House" that had stood on the site. The experience of watching that house go up in flames may well have been a factor in Palmer's decision to adopt a design that incorporated design advances in fire prevention.

According to archaeological findings, Palmer's "Exceeding good Brick House two Stories high" was slightly larger than the building it replaced. It contained a side passage (hallway) like the Tayloe House that extended from front to back. The passage was generously proportioned, with a staircase to the second floor, doors to the hall and a chamber, and enough room left over that it was a useful living space. The upper level consists of three chambers and another wide passage.

The street facade of the house featured three bays, with the entrance at one end. But a brick extension was constructed in 1857 by its owner, a prominent merchant named William W. Vest. The result was a radical transformation: the house suddenly assumed the look of a classic, five-bay colonial. Dormers were added to the roof, the windows enlarged, and the building effectively doubled in size. It was a generous home, even by Victorian standards, and visiting military leaders soon took good advantage. During the Civil War, it became headquarters for Confederate General Joseph Johnston and, literally the day after Johnston vacated, Union General George B. McClellan. In an 1862 letter home to his wife, McClellan described the spoils of war: "This is a beautiful town; several very old houses, pretty gardens. I have taken possession of a very fine old house," he continued, "which Joe Johnston occupied as headquarters. It has a lovely flower garden, and conservatory. If you were here, I would be much inclined to spend some time here."

Restoration of the house to its eighteenth-century appearance was done in 1952. Vest's nineteenth-century extension was demolished, as was an enclosed porch. The dormers were removed, appropriate windows reinstalled, and the brickwork cleaned, removing layers of whitewash and paint. While the exterior looks much as it did in John Palmer's time, little original fabric inside other than the stair survived the Victorian renovation, one reason the house is not an exhibition house but a private residence. ◁▷

FACING PAGE: It is a three-bay brick house, but with the same, compact side-passage plan as the wood-frame Tayloe and Lightfoot houses (see pages 54 and 106, respectively).

TOP AND FACING PAGE: The gracious front steps seem to swoop upward to the house. All but the bottom stair survived from the eighteenth century, but the profile of the missing step was identified by archaeologists and restored.

The doghouselike wooden structure at the far end of the front elevation is a bulkhead that allows access to the basement. It was reconstructed based on archaeological findings and physical evidence that survived in the brick wall.

TOP, LEFT: The lunette window in the gable was rediscovered when the 1857 addition was removed.

TOP, RIGHT: Yes, that is a void in the brickwork. Called a "put-log" hole, it was one of many fixing points for scaffolding timbers the masons used during construction. Left unfilled for almost twenty years after the house was completed, the put-log holes were once again opened by the restorers when they returned the house to its prerevolutionary appearance.

BOTTOM: The gable roof is steep, though in an equivalent English house of the time, it would likely have been three or even three-and-a-half stories tall.

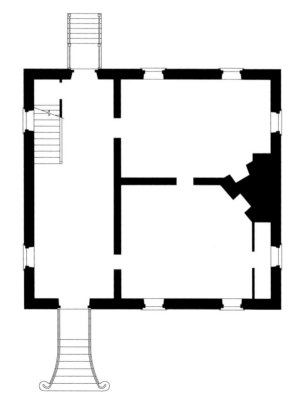

0   15
FEET

TOP, LEFT: The masons who built the house had to make their own wedge-shaped bricks to build the so-called jack arches over the windows and doors. The flattened arches were formed by using rubbed bricks that were fabricated on-site by abrading bricks against a stone or other bricks.

TOP, RIGHT: The sophisticated brickwork included a molded ledge, or "water table," that served to shed water away from the foundation and to add a plinth to the building for decorative effect.

BOTTOM: The floor plan suggests the efficiency of the house's design. The generous passage is usable as living spaces on the first and second floors, while the chimney mass was located so a single chimney served the hall and chamber.

TOP: Such utilitarian elements as the raised panels on the door, the H-hinge, and the baseboard have in our time taken on added aesthetic appeal.

BOTTOM: Today the first-floor passage doubles as a hallway *and* a sitting room with bookcases and chairs.

The one chimney mass in the house was set in the midst of the west wall, allowing for angled fire-places in the principal rooms, including this parlor with its reproduction floor–to–ceiling chimney paneling.

FACING PAGE: The door
to the rear yard is less
grand than the entrance,
compressed as it is by the
stairway.

Palmer's house originally
consisted of three bays. A
century later, a local merchant added two more bays,
making the place almost
unrecognizable. Another
century passed before
Palmer's original vision
was restored.

William Lightfoot House

DUKE OF GLOUCESTER STREET
CONSTRUCTED BEFORE 1782

For nearly a century, the Lightfoot family owned two adjacent lots on Duke of Gloucester Street. Which of the Lightfoots built the house there has not been established, but almost certainly it was one of two Williams, father and son, who owned the house from 1751 until 1809. In either case, the house existed by 1782, since it was recorded in that year on the Frenchman's Map.

The elder and the younger William Lightfoot were merchants, based in Jamestown, who traveled frequently to Williamsburg on matters of business and politics (the father served in the colonial House of Burgesses, the son in the House of Delegates). They probably used this house as John Tayloe used his Williamsburg home, as a *pied à terre* accommodation for visits to the capital (see Tayloe House, page 54).

The Lightfoot and Tayloe houses have more in common than the uses to which they were put in the eighteenth century. Both are wood-frame houses with gambrel roofs. In addition, the houses share a common plan, with a through passage on one side of the house that contains the stairs as well as entrances to the two principal first-floor rooms, originally a hall and chamber. The Palmer House is a brick example of such a side-passage plan (see page 96). Despite such similarities, the Lightfoot house has its unique characteristics, as it measures thirty-one feet front to back, making it three feet deeper than it is wide, and the lower pitch of its roof is unusually steep.

In the nineteenth century, new owners updated the house, adding a two-story wing to the east side and applying a porch to the front. The porch reflected changes in social patterns in the nineteenth century—people began to spend leisure time on porches overlooking the street—while the addition housed the law offices of the owner who had acquired the house in 1847. These changes were obliterated in 1931, when the house was reworked. At that time the house was adapted for twentieth-century residents (it remains today a private home). Along with utilities, a modern kitchen, bath, closets, and pantry were inserted. But much original material remains inside, while the exterior was restored to give it the same appearance on the Duke of Gloucester streetscape that one—or perhaps both—of the William Lightfoots would have known. ◉

FACING PAGE: Small but stately, the house faces north on busy Duke of Gloucester Street.

TOP: Before its restoration in 1931, the house had a porch across its original facade and a two-story wing on its east end. These and other modifications were undone to return the house to its eighteenth-century appearance.

BOTTOM: The roof encloses a second floor with spaces nearly equal to that of the ground level.

FACING PAGE: In the unusual proportions of the house—it is deeper than it is wide—is a lesson learned then and often useful even today about adapting the footprint of a house to reflect its setting, in this case a dense cityscape.

TOP: The entrance porch along Duke of Gloucester Street, with its Chinese Chippendale railing

BOTTOM, LEFT: The builder's art in the eighteenth century relied upon molding planes, as evidenced by the raised panels on the door, the molded door frame, and the beaded weatherboards. The assemblage of moldings make for a subtle sculptural quality, with surface changes and shadows adding visual interest.

BOTTOM, RIGHT: A louvered blind could be used for security or for protection from the sun.

TOP: The rear (south) elevation of the house features an eight-foot by ten-foot porch. While there was no archaeological evidence that such a porch existed, it provides shade and rain protection to the principal entrance for today's inhabitants.

BOTTOM: Sometimes called a "town-house plan," this arrangement of side passage, parlor, and chamber was adapted in 1931, when a kitchen and closets were inserted into what had been the first-floor chamber. Upstairs a bath was added at the front of the house in the passage.

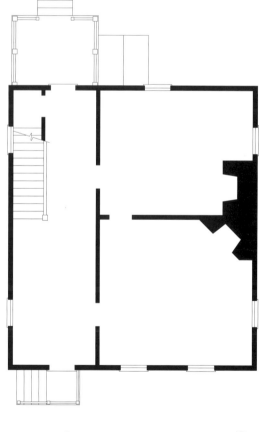

FEET

St. George Tucker House

NICHOLSON STREET

CONSTRUCTED 1718–19; UPDATED CA. 1750; RELOCATED 1788
RENOVATED 1788–95, CA. 1845 AND 1890

Perhaps the St. George Tucker House is the equivalent of a final exam, one administered by a benign old professor. The Tucker house certainly makes the puzzles posed by the other dwellings described in this book seem like mere quizzes. Yet upon understanding the various conundrums the Tucker house presented its restorers, a larger sense of Williamsburg's past emerges. *Where'd he get that problem?* the student might ask upon leaving the classroom. *Must've taken the old guy a while to invent that one!*

The Tucker house, of course, is far from imaginary. It began as a center passage, hall-and-chamber house built for a man named William Levingston who built the first theater in America next door to this house. The dwelling was impressive for its day—it was built in 1718–19, rising near John Brush's house (see Thomas Everard House, page 36)—and the location was significant, too, as it overlooked Palace Green. A later owner, George Gilmer, was a prominent and prosperous Williamsburg doctor and apothecary who served as Williamsburg's mayor for a time as well as in several other public offices. He felt he needed more space, so he added a new wing and updated the house in the 1750s, installing, among other refinements, paneling where previously plain plaster had covered the walls. But all of that is just the prologue for the much longer tale of the house after it came into the hands of St. George Tucker and four generations of his descendants. Those same descendants preserved not only the house but also exten-

sive records—including contracts, accounts, and sketches—that amount to the best documentary record for any eighteenth-century house in Williamsburg.

The Bermuda-born St. George Tucker had come to town in 1770 as a student. He studied at the College of William and Mary, saw military service during the revolution, and read law with George Wythe (see George Wythe House, page 44). He assumed Wythe's post as professor of law at his alma mater in 1790, and later served as a state and federal judge. His 1803 edition of Blackstone's *Commentaries*, an indispensable law text, became the American standard. As a public man, he needed a suitable residence; but his family obligations, too, played a role in the evolution of this house, which he purchased in 1788.

By then the focus of Williamsburg had changed, as it was no longer Virginia's capital, and the Governor's Palace had burned in 1781, meaning Palace Green had become just another address. The life of the town had shifted, so less than a fortnight after gaining title to the house, Tucker contracted mason Humphrey Harwood to build a new foundation and carpenter John Saunders to move the house. By relocating the structure a short distance to the southeast and turning it ninety degrees, they reoriented the dwelling to Market Square, the new focus of activity in the town.

Tucker was a widower with five young children; he soon remarried and his new wife, Lelia, was a widow with two children

FACING PAGE: The house reflects a mix of times—the trim is colonial in style, the colors those of ca. 1798, but the house retains the dormers added in the nineteenth century.

TOP: The rear elevation, seen from an adjoining garden

BOTTOM: Within the central mass of the house is the original structure. It was lower, shallower, and constructed around the corner, but much of the skeleton of the earlier dwelling survives beneath the skin of multiple remodeling and restoration efforts.

of her own. Over a half-dozen years, Tucker's ambitious building campaign would subsume the original structure. By 1795 the roof of the main house had been raised to two stories. East and west wings had been added, along with a shed addition to the north, and Gilmer's staircase moved. New chimneys, new interior finishes, and a kitchen and connecting covered walkway were added. The original three-room, 18½-by-40-foot structure had tripled in length, doubled in depth, and contained some ten rooms on the first floor.

Much later, Tucker's son, Nathaniel Beverley Tucker, introduced his share of modifications. He raised the roofs of both wings and added dormers in about 1845, and, like his father, moved the staircase. He also added a chimney and another partition to create double parlors, and had the trim on the house reworked in the then-popular Grecian style. The next generation of owners, Cynthia Tucker Coleman and her husband, Dr. Charles W. Coleman, turned the east wing into an apartment in the 1890s. Their son added bathrooms after he took up residence in 1907. The house was restored in 1930–31 by Colonial Williamsburg, a process in which a mix of early and later structures was given a colonial revival updating. The result was a charming, meandering house with an overall look that represented no time in particular but was a minor monument to changing tastes.

❧ ❧ ❧

The house before its 1931 restoration

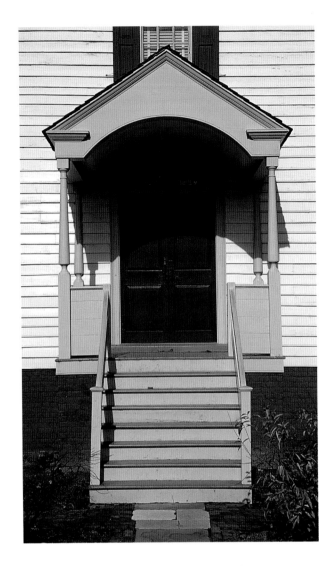

TOP, LEFT: The needs of different times are reflected in every home. Even at a museum restoration such as Colonial Williamsburg, a family's personal wishes sometimes were expressed architecturally. The sheltering porch here is a reproduction, built at the request of the family who, having gifted the house to Colonial Williamsburg, was granted life tenancy.

TOP, RIGHT: The trim on the pedimented dormers is 1930s colonial while the dormers themselves date from ca. 1845.

MIDDLE: A nine-over-nine light window in one of the ca. 1792 wings

BOTTOM: The floor plan as elaborated by St. George Tucker himself, ca. 1795

FACING PAGE: From the front door, looking north through the passage into the rear parlor, or "great hall" as it was renamed during the 1931 renovation

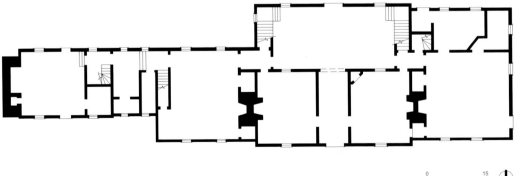

0   15
FEET

Unlike most eighteenth-century homes of Colonial Williamsburg, the St. George Tucker House has not had its calendar reversed. Or, at least, not entirely. The peculiar nature of this house has made it a unique challenge to its restorers. In the same way, it makes a revealing case study for the workings of historic preservation at Colonial Williamsburg.

When the Coleman family, descendants of St. George Tucker, deeded the house to Colonial Williamsburg in 1930, a life tenancy agreement was part of the understanding. It was not practical then to return the house to its prerevolutionary appearance, although the stated period of interpretation at Colonial Williamsburg is the 1770s; that would have necessitated the demolition of most of the house (recall that until 1788, the house consisted of just the three original rooms built for Levingston in 1719). Instead of aiming to restore the place to a specific time in its history, an interpretive restoration was undertaken. The goal in those days was less a matter of reaching a precise understanding of the eighteenth century. The less rigorous goal, stated simply, was to capture something of the spirit of the time. Only after the death of St. George Tucker's great-great-granddaughter, Dr. Janet Kimbrough, did the Architectural Research Department get the opportunity to delve more deeply and investigate in systematic fashion St. George Tucker's rambling house and to try to relate its findings to the voluminous documentary evidence of the building process from St. George Tucker's time.

Thanks in part to new techniques not available to the earlier restorers, the 1994–95 investigation produced important revelations. A building chronology was developed, establishing when doors, moldings, dormers, partitions, mantels, porches, and other elements had been introduced or removed. It became clear that more than a few misunderstandings had guided the 1930s restoration.

One of the most important concerned the tall, triple-sash windows in the two front rooms of the main block. The depression-era restorers not only removed them but also discarded them under the misapprehension that they dated not from St. George Tucker's time but had come later.

The richness of the surviving written record and its relationship to the artifact itself was demonstrated by one aspect of the study in particular. The point of origin was an extraordinary document that survived from 1798. A master painter in Williamsburg, Jeremiah Satterwhite, agreed on August 30 of that year to paint Mr. Tucker's house. The understanding reached was memorialized in a contract that detailed the scope of the work (the inside and outside of the house were to get two coats of paint) and the payment due (Satterwhite's fee was to be $50). Even more valuable to the investigators were the further details enumerated in the agreement. Tucker was to provide the ladders and two-hundred-forty pounds of "white Lead" paint, along with one hundred pounds each of "Spanish brown" and "Yellow Ochre." Satterwhite would bring his own brushes and pots for boiling the paint. The color scheme was enumerated in detail—outside it would be Spanish brown for the roof, "pure white" for the body color, and "Chocolate Colour" for the foundations; inside, more chocolate for the trim and stone or straw for the walls. Paint analysis conducted in the 1990s corroborated the contract, affirming that Satterwhite had indeed done as he was contracted to do. Thus, a workman's contract proved an invaluable tool in the restoration process. And the exhaustive study produced a new understanding of a house that is among Williamsburg's most complex.

The 1990s investigation was accompanied by a miscellany of modernizing and restoration tasks. The exterior paint scheme of 1798 was restored. A handicapped-accessible bathroom was installed to meet the requirements of the Americans with Disabilities Act. Electrical and mechanical systems were brought up to date. And the house was adapted for use as Colonial Williamsburg's donor reception center. Today, contributors to the Foundation find a relaxed setting for light refreshments and a respite from walking the streets of Colonial Williamsburg.

Like Williamsburg itself, the St. George Tucker House has become a place where the past and the present have come to a remarkable accommodation. ⚜

FACING PAGE: The stacked gable ends, seen from behind the hedgerow west of the house, make a sculptural composition.

The east wing, added in the 1791–92 remodeling, was 33-feet deep and originally housed a large bedchamber and two small dressing rooms. In the way of evolving houses, the second floor dormers and bedroom came later.

Afterword

History does not march. That may be a convenient political metaphor with overtones of progress but, in truth, time and history are forever in flux. Change is the rule and at places like Colonial Williamsburg, time has gone backward.

Or, more accurately, it goes back and forth. One of the ironies of life at Colonial Williamsburg is that while the calendar has been stopped, the learning about the years just before the American Revolution has not. The place is not simply frozen in the 1770s, its chosen time of interpretation. As each generation of researchers learns more—and, in general, tries to interfere less with the past—a more accurate historical view emerges. In no arena is this evolution in understanding more apparent than in the town's architecture and, in particular, in its houses.

Just as the interpretation of the past at Colonial Williamsburg has evolved, so has its approach to looking at and presenting its buildings. You might think that a building reworked by the Goodwin-Rockefeller generation had given up all its secrets, but that simply is not so. With advances in technology, much can be gleaned from restored buildings, even those stripped of original plaster and, along with it, countless clues and details. If connoisseurship once dominated, technology has become a check and balance: dendrochronology, paint analysis, and other scientific modes of investigation have added the quantitative to the qualitative.

In visiting Colonial Williamsburg, the sense of history is palpable. In a way, to go there is to visit the past: it is hardly accidental that typing "history.org" into a search engine will take you to the Colonial Williamsburg Foundation Web site. Much of the architectural fabric of the town survived when Messieurs Goodwin and Rockefeller launched their venture; in the three-quarters of a century since the founding of Colonial Williamsburg, countless signs of nineteenth-century life have been erased. Yet Colonial Williamsburg is not the past, of course; nor is it simply a stage set.

Perhaps a more accurate way to regard Colonial Williamsburg is as a place where you can see history being formulated. And that's just as true today, more than seventy-five years after the large-scale work of restoration was begun. The findings come in fits and starts. It has become apparent that the initial restoration efforts at Williamsburg were too hurried—twenty-five major buildings were completed in the first half-dozen years. The restorers then were doing the job the "right" way in terms of their time, but today some aspects of their approach seem rushed. And there are regrets at the undocumented reuse of various elements in some houses, which blurs the distinctions between different eras and locales.

With each generation, then, the historians, interpreters, and curators at Colonial Williamsburg gain new insights into the distant past and the misunderstandings of the more recent past. Since they cannot go all the way back to visit—nor can we, really—the ongoing historical and cultural quest for understanding offers us the best available glimpse of the past. Colonial Williamsburg is a place where some people experience the first brush with history. And each of its houses, complete with its stories and inhabitants, helps humanize the place and the life of the eighteenth century.

Glossary

ARCHITRAVE In classical architecture, the lowest portion of the *entablature* set immediately upon the columns or *pilasters* (originally, the architrave was the structural beam spanning the distance from column to column). Also: an ornamental *molding* covering the joints between the frame of a window or door opening and the surrounding wall surface (see also *cornice* and *frieze*).

BAY Unit of space between the principal vertical framing members.

BEAD A round, convex molding, often found on paneling and the trim around doorways and windows.

BEAM Main horizontal structural member in the construction of a frame house.

CHAIR BOARD Interior, horizontal molding fastened at waist height to protect wall surfaces. Today, often called a chair rail and, in Great Britain, a dado.

CHAMBER In eighteenth-century Williamsburg, a room generally given over to sleeping.

CHAMFER Bevel of approximately 45 degrees put on a previously square-cut corner of a beam or other wooden member.

CLAPBOARD In eighteenth-century Virginia, a thin, tapering, split board, used as a roofing and walling surface, typically four to five feet in length (see also *weatherboarding*).

CORINTHIAN Order of architecture characterized by capitals decorated with carved acanthus leaves.

CORNER BOARD Vertical exterior trim board at the corner of a house.

CORNICE Band at the top of the classical *entablature* that projects at the crown of a wall (see also *architrave* and *frieze*).

COURSE Horizontal row of bricks, shingles, stones, or other building material.

DEED Signed legal document that conveys or transfers ownership of land.

DENTIL One of a row of small blocks projecting from a cornice (see also *modillion*).

DORIC Order of architecture characterized by its simple capitals without the carved acanthus leaves of the *corinthian* or the scrolls of the *ionic*.

DOUBLE-HUNG WINDOW Window in which the two sashes slide up and down within the plane of the wall.

DOUBLE PILE House plan in which the building is two rooms deep.

ELEVATION Architectural drawing indicating how completed interior or exterior walls will look; the point of view is that of an observer looking from a horizontal vantage.

ENTABLATURE In the orders of classical architecture, the assemblage of the horizontal bands of the *cornice, frieze*, and *architrave*, the elements immediately above (and supported by) the columns and capitals.

FABRIC The physical material of a building; the implication is of the interweaving between the various component materials.

FANLIGHT Semicircular or half-elliptical window sash, often located over a doorway.

FENESTRATION The arrangement and proportioning of the openings (windows and doors) in a building.

FRAME HOUSE A house in which the structural parts are wood or depend upon a wood frame for support.

FRIEZE Horizontal band between the *cornice* and the *architrave* in the *entablature* in classical architecture.

GABLE End wall of a building formed by the eave line of a double-sloped roof in the shape of an inverted *V.*

HALL In eighteenth-century Williamsburg, a multipurpose first-floor room originally for cooking, eating, entertaining, and sleeping in modest two- and three-room homes. As service and sleeping activities were relegated to other places later in the century, the hall gradually came to be referred to as the parlor. The use of the word hall as a term applied to a corridor developed in the next century.

HEADER Brick laid with its end outward.

HIP ROOF A gable roof with the ends shortened to form sloping triangular surfaces.

IONIC Order of architecture identifiable by the carved volutes (scrolls) of its capitals.

JAMB Side or head lining of a window, door, or other opening.

JOIST Horizontal beam in a frame house that supports floor boards and/or ceiling surfaces.

LATH Strips of wood nailed to the frame of the building to support plaster or shingles.

MANTELPIECE The decorative frame around the fireplace, whether made of wood or stone.

MASONRY Brick, concrete, stone, or other materials bonded together with mortar to form walls, piers, buttresses, or other masses.

MODILLION Ornamental blocks or brackets applied in series to the *soffit,* or underside of a *cornice.*

MOLDINGS Strips of wood used for finish or decorative purposes with regular channels or projections that provide transitions from one surface or material to another (e.g., baseboard, *chair board,* or *cornice* moldings).

MORTISE Cavity cut into the side or end of one framing member that forms a joint with a tenon cut into the end of a second member.

MUNTIN Small wooden pieces that provide the divisions between the individual panes of glass in a window sash.

NEWEL Large post at the top, bottom, turns, or landing of a stairway.

OGEE Molding consisting of a double curve.

ORDERS The various combinations of vertical (columns or *pilasters*) and horizontal elements (*entablature*) that distinguish the structure of a classical building (see also *corinthian, doric,* and *ionic*).

PANELING Wall surface consisting of panels set within a framework of vertical stiles and horizontal rails.

PARLOR A multipurpose first-floor room that in early-eighteenth-century Williamsburg houses was used as a sleeping space; in two-room plans, the name was often interchangeable with *chamber*. Over the decades, "parlor" replaced the word *hall* in designating a formal sitting room used for entertaining.

PASSAGE In eighteenth-century Williamsburg, the space, usually extending front to back, that provided access to the rooms. Also used as a waiting space for visitors and as a "summer hall" (see also *chamber, hall,* and *parlor*).

PEDIMENT Shallow, triangular area formed at the gable end of a roof by the two roof lines, echoing the temple end of a classical structure. A pedimented headpiece is sometimes found over doors and windows.

PILASTER Flattened column affixed to a wall and projecting only slightly from it.

PLANTER Person who owned a plantation and who was of a certain elevated social class; or, one who derived his principal income from growing crops.

PLATE Horizontal structural member that caps a wall structure and supports the rafters in a *frame house*.

POST Principal vertical structural member in a *frame house*.

PUT-LOG HOLE A void in a masonry wall used as a fixing point for scaffolding timbers.

QUOIN Decorative projecting stone (or wooden elements carved to resemble stone) at the corner of a building.

RAFTER One of a series of inclined structural members that support the roof, running from the exterior wall to the ridge.

SASH Single, light frame that holds the glass in a window unit and is designed to slide vertically in a track.

SIDELIGHT One of a pair of windows flanking a door.

SIDING Finished surface of exterior walls (see also *weatherboarding* and *clapboard*).

SILL Lowermost structural member of a *frame house*, the sill is the large-dimension wooden element that rests directly on the foundation and forms its perimeter.

SINGLE PILE House plan in which the building is one-room deep.

SOFFIT The underside of an overhanging *cornice*; also called a corona when used in context of a classical cornice.

STRETCHER Brick laid lengthwise.

STUD Secondary vertical wooden structural member used as a supporting element in walls or partitions.

TENON Tongue-shaped projection at the end of a framing member that fits into a *mortise*.

UNDERTAKER A builder or contractor; in eighteenth-century parlance, one who undertook the construction of a building.

VERNACULAR Guileless, unpretentious buildings erected with local materials and labor guided by local tradition rather than national or international trends.

WEATHERBOARDING Overlapping horizontal wooden cladding, fixed to the exterior of a wood-frame structure; generally longer, thicker, and more stylish than cruder *clapboards*. Typically weatherboards are of sawn rather than split stock and often have a molded lower edge.

For Further Reading

Many authors, knowingly and not, contributed to this book. Some provided hard facts, others softer matters to muse upon. I commend the books and articles listed below to anyone wishing to learn more.

The gentlemen in the Architectural Research Department were so kind as to share with me the updates incorporated into the forthcoming revision of Marcus Whiffin's classic *The Eighteenth-Century Houses of Williamsburg*, long the bible for anyone wishing to understand Williamsburg's domestic architecture. George H. Yetter's *Williamsburg Before and After: The Rebirth of Virginia's Colonial Capital* (Williamsburg, Va.: The Colonial Williamsburg Foundation, 1988) is a delightful saunter through time. Dell Upton's book, *Holy Things and Profane: Anglican Parish Churches in Colonial Virginia* (New Haven, Conn.: Yale University Press, 1986) and *The Transformation of Virginia, 1740–1790* by Rhys Isaac (Chapel Hill: The University of North Carolina Press, 1982) are also essential texts when thinking and writing about eighteenth-century Virginia. For architectural terminology, the invaluable reference is *An Illustrated Glossary of Early Southern Architecture and Landscape*, Carl R. Lounsbury, ed. (Charlottesville: University Press of Virginia, 1994). *Creating Colonial Williamsburg* by Anders Greenspan (Washington, D.C.: Smithsonian Institution Press, 2002) helps put the twentieth-century restoration at Williamsburg into an historiographical perspective.

Perhaps more difficult to find but certainly no less valuable are a number of essays that have appeared in periodical form. Two watershed essays stand out in particular: Mark R. Wenger's "The Central Passage in Virginia: Evolution of an Eighteenth-Century Living Space" in *Perspectives in Vernacular Architecture, II*, Camille Wells, editor (Columbia: University of Missouri Press, 1986); and Dell Upton's "Vernacular Domestic Architecture in Eighteenth-Century Virginia" (*Winterthur Portfolio*, vol. 17, nos. 2/3, 1982). A miscellany of other writings offer important insights on individual houses. Among them are Edward A. Chappell's "Understanding Williamsburg's Houses," *The Colonial Williamsburg Interpreter* (vol. 15, no. 2, 1994); Margaret Beck Pritchard's and Willie Graham's article "Rethinking Two Houses at Colonial Williamsburg" in *The Magazine Antiques*, vol. 157, no. 1 (January 1996), pp. 166–75; Mark R. Wenger's essay, "Investigations at the Brush-Everard House" in *The Colonial Williamsburg Interpreter* (vol. 15, no.1, 1994); Edward A. Chappell's "The Changing Complexion of Thomas Everard's House," *Colonial Williamsburg* (winter, 1995–96); Mark R. Wenger's essays in *The Early Architecture of Tidewater Virginia: A Guidebook for the Twenty-Third Annual Vernacular Architecture Forum Conference* (Williamsburg, Va.: Architectural Research Department, Colonial Williamsburg Foundation, 2002) and "The Benjamin Powell House" in *The Colonial Williamsburg Interpreter* (vol. 14, no. 3, 1993). From the 1999 special edition of *The Colonial Williamsburg Interpreter* (vol. 20, no. 3), devoted to the latest restoration of the Peyton Randolph House, two essays in particular relate to the architectural revelations, namely "An Overview: Re-Translating the Past" by Edward A. Chappell and "A House Befitting Mr. Attorney" by William Graham. In learning about the St. George Tucker House, the standard reference has become *St. George Tucker House: An Architectural Analysis* by Roberta G. Laynor, Carl R. Lounsbury, and Mark R. Wenger (Williamsburg, Va.: Colonial Williamsburg Foundation, 2002).

Index

Page numbers in **bold** indicate illustrations.